A CELTIC
CHRISTMAS

A CELTIC
CHRISTMAS

*Classic Tales
from the
Emerald Isle*

Edited by Mairtin O' Griofa
Illustrated by Sheila Kern

Sterling Publishing Co., Inc.   New York
A STERLING/MAIN STREET BOOK

Library of Congress Cataloging-in-Publication Data

A Celtic Christmas : classic tales from the Emerald Isle / edited by
  Mairtin O' Griofa : illustrated by Sheila Kern.
      p.   cm.
    "A Sterling / Main Street book."
    Includes index.
    ISBN 0-8069-9586-6
    1. Christmas-Ireland. 2. Ireland-Social life and customs.
  1. O' Griofa, Mairtin.
  GT4987. 467. C45 1996
  394 . 2 ' 663 ' 09415-dc20   96-20874
                                                              CIP

Designed by John Murphy
Assisted by Edmond Smith and Eric Greif
Typeset by Upper Case Limited, Cork, Ireland

10   9   8   7   6   5   4

A Sterling/Main Street Book

Published in 1996 by Sterling Publishing Company, Inc.
387 Park Avenue South, New York, N.Y. 10016
© 1996 by Sterling Publishing Company, Inc.
Distributed in Canada by Sterling Publishing
c/o Canadian Manda Group, One Atlantic Avenue, Suite 105
Toronto, Ontario, Canada M6K 3E7
Distributed in Great Britain and Europe by Cassell PLC
Wellington House, 125 Strand, London WC2R OBB, England
Distributed in Australia by Capricorn Link (Australia) Pty Ltd.
P.O. Box 6651, Baulkham Hills, Business Centre, NSW 2153,
Australia

Manufactured in the United States of America
All rights reserved

ISBN 0-8069-9586-6

Contents

Introduction   7

Galway Jack's Christmas *by Teresa Brayton*   11

The Ballymaconkey Christmas Club *by Ivan Adair*   22

Percy's Christmas Party *by L. R. Henry*   31

The Compact *by P. D. Murphy*   39

Christmas Roses *by Evelyn Cuthbert*   47

McWhistler's Mix Up *by L. A. Finn*   57

Barney Broderick's Close Shave *by Sean McElvoy*   67

The Christmas Raffle *by Reardon Connor*   72

One Christmas Eve *by Madeline Cummins*   77

Mr. & Mrs. Santa Claus *by Anonymous*   90

Widow Dennehy's Christmas Visitors *by L. Sullivan*   98

The Miser's Reward *by B. J. K. Quinn*   109

Gobble, Gobble *by M. Redican*   117

The Black Dog *by Dee Culan*   123

Index   128

Introduction

PERHAPS NOWHERE IN THE WORLD is the old homely festival of Christmas celebrated so much with its time-honored joyousness and homeliness as in Ireland. Despite the materialism of the age, and the matter-of-fact trend of thought that typifies the rising generations, Christmas is still associated in Irish minds with much of the old fervor of faith and with much of the old adherence to custom and tradition that cling round the name of Yule in Irish songs and stories. Many of the old beliefs and superstitions have, of course, sunk into the grave of oblivion, unwept, unhonored, if not altogether unsung, before the more "enlightened" spirit of our day; and it is only in places remote from town and city that such now survive. But Christmas is a time of memories, and back to the past will fancy glide, when around the Yuletido fire the faces of family and friends gather.

The Irish heart especially seems to be a storehouse of memories; and as such it is often seen in the Christmas household lore reflected in many of the Irish Yuletide stories that follow.

Christmas is so associated with feasting and hospitality that, naturally, many domestic superstitions are connected with it. In many parts of Europe it is thought that bread and cakes baked at this season have special virtues, a belief dating from when white bread and cakes were luxuries, only to be indulged in on "high days and holidays."

Many Irish people remember the times when country folk rarely ate bakers' bread except at Christmas and Easter.

The Irish still bake their great barmbracks for Christmas, though the custom of bakers and grocers presenting their customers with them has long died out. In times past in some parts of Cork and Kerry it was customary for the "vanithee" on Twelfth Day to take out a round cake of hastable-bread and throw it against the house-door, crying: "I wish hunger, or starvation to the Sassenach," or to some other province, county, or parish in Ireland! This was supposed to secure plenty and prosperity to the woman's own district for the year. It was not a very kindly or charitable custom with which to wind up the season of peace and good-will, but very few women now "break the cake against the door," even in the most remote districts on "The Women's Christmas," as Twelfth Day is often called.

Barmbracks still figure in the menu on this festival, when so many social gatherings take place in Ireland, but gone are the days when, in the country, matches were often arranged as the young folks amused themselves with games and dancing, and the old folks sat by the ruddy turf-fire. Once the "Little Christmas Cake" in towns generally contained a ring, coin, and pea, or bean, as well as a bit of stick. The last is said to indicate that the finder will be doomed to single blessedness, while the ring means early matrimony, the coin, wealth, and the bean or pea, good luck. In former days in Ireland bits of rag were put into the cake – blue for a sailor, red for a soldier, green for a policeman, and black for a widower, while a straw was put in for a farmer.

There is a widespread idea that clothes should not be washed, rooms swept, or beds turned on Christmas Day, and naturally all unnecessary work is avoided on this great festival. In the Tyrol women fancy the mice would eat any thread they spun during the Yuletide holidays. The custom of giving a thorough cleaning to the house before the festival is very general; even in the days when many country folk lived in the most wretched mud cabins, it was usual for poor women to tidy them as far as it was possible "for the Christmas." In the days when enormous fires were lighted, and great yule-logs blazed on upon hearths, it was usual to have all chimneys swept before the festive season, in case of fires. Electric light and matches have almost killed the superstition that it was unlucky to give away light or fire at Christmas, but in some parts of the country it is still thought lucky to breakfast by candlelight on Christmas and New Year's morning. In bygone days a tinderbox, live coal, or a sod of burning turf could not be borrowed for love or money during "the Twelve Days," lest the luck of the house should go with them. In the South and West the Irish still have their Christmas candles – the great tapers often weighing over a pound – which are lit on Christmas Eve, and are supposed to burn all night, as ill-luck is said to befall the dwelling where the big candle is extinguished before the wintry dawn breaks on Christmas Day.

In some places it is said that one should wear something new at Christmas, as well as at Easter, or new garments will be few in the coming year. It is said to be unlucky to wear a ragged article of clothing on Christmas Day – a hole means a leak in the purse – but should a garment be torn on the festival it must not be sewn up. Christmas needlework is unlucky – it can be pinned together instead, for pins are very lucky at Yuletide. Some say this is because they represent the sharp thorns of the holly; others give a commonsense explanation, and declare the belief dates from the time when these useful implements were a luxury and were given as Christmas and New Year gifts. At one period they were only sold in shops on the first and second of January, so women were given "pin-money" for their purchase at the beginning of the year; the name was afterwards bestowed on sums allowed for a woman's personal expenses. Anything pinned to the clothing is suposed to be lucky at Christmas, especially a sprig of holly or mistletoe. There was an old belief that one should never refuse a mince-pie at Christmas, and in order to secure twelve happy months in the new year one should be out in a dozen different houses during the holidays. It was also supposed to be lucky to taste plum-pudding in other dwellings besides one's own at this season, while even the most dyspeptic people were advised to taste the blazing holly-crowned pudding on Christmas Day "for luck."

If the Irish were to do all the things their great-grandparents believed brought them luck during the Christmas season and after, they would have a very busy time of it. For there is scarcely one custom connected with the festive season that has not a host of good-fortune-bringing ideas attached to it.

The Irish can't even stir the Christmas pudding without "leaving out the luck" if they do it in the wrong way. In the old days each member of the family was expected to give a "stir" to the plum pudding. Clockwise was the correct direction; stirred in this way, greater pressure was supposed to be brought to bear from east to west and this commemorated the journey of the Wise Men from the East. Evidently left-handed helpers would have to reverse their usual practice on these occasions.

Twelve eggs is the correct number to use if one wishes the pudding to be a "lucky" one (one for every month of the year) and not less than twelve ingredients must go to make it. Silver charms must be hidden in the pudding to be eaten on Christmas Day and the excitement of finding out from them what one's luck will be for the coming year.

And what about the large share of legend connected with the mince-pies?

In the dim past they were not round but oblong in shape, and were meant to represent the manger where the infant Christ was born. Everything that goes to the making of a mince-pie has a connection with the story of the Wise Men. The candied peel represents the gold offered by one Eastern King, the mace stands for the frankincense, the cinnamon the myrrh.

The fourteen stories that follow are sentimental, intelligent, touching, supernatural, instilled with Yuletide customs, and lubricated with gallons of alcoholic drink – very Irish indeed.

Galway Jack's Christmas

❧

I T WAS THE EVENING before Christmas Eve. A black frost was holding the countryside in its bitter grip, even the leafless trees seemed to be huddling their naked boughs closer together as if seeking comfort from the raking wind that went charging over hills and hollows. It was no night to be outdoors, if one had a warm hearth to sit beside, and so decided Tom Fahy as he finished up his last few tasks of the evening and gave a parting look around to see if he had left everything in order for the night. The cows were bedded down, the calves fed, the two horses content in their stalls; silence lay over the pig sties and the hen houses at the back of the barn, even Shep, the watchful collie, was sleeping warmly in his kennel after an unusually active day about the place. With a mind at ease Tom Fahy burst into his favorite come-all-ye:

"If you'll give me your lily-white hand and say you'll be my bride, for you I'll plough and sow, down by the Shannon side."

As he lifted the latch Mrs. Fahy greeted him with stormy words: "Come in out of the cold for goodness sake, Tom, or do you want to be freezin' the marrow in your bones! Singin', indeed, on a night like this with the wind tearing by that would cut the horns off a goat! Anyway, it isn't an old dronthaun like you should be singin' but a blessed hymn, considerin' the time that's in it. 'Give me your lily-white hand,' indeed! It's too bad you didn't get someone with that same to marry you instead of myself with the two hands never done workin'. Fine help to you a white-fingered lassie would be and you mowin' and ploughin', anyway. It's many a time you'd be wantin' a lift with the work for all she'd do, barrin' look pretty, and maybe strokin' the cat's back to show off her

11

lily-white hands. Into the corner there with you while I make the tea and drive the cold out of your bones."

Tom Fahy slipped into his warm corner by the fire, stretching his hands towards the pleasant heat. The busier Mary was the more her tongue wagged, sometimes, and tonight she was up to her eyes in great preparation for the coming festival. The kitchen was redolent of baking and boiling good things for Christmas where a ham had just been lifted out of the pot still steaming by the table, a big brown barmbrack cake was tilted against the wall with currants and raisins sticking out of it as if there wasn't room for them all inside, a yellow bowl was full of some mysterious mixture that spoke of a plum pudding being in progress. Tom sniffed at the enticing odors and felt that life was good.

You're a fine woman, Mary," he said, " but you have one bad fault; you don't like my singin' anymore, and that's a sure sign your love is coolin' off from what it used to be. I mind the time when you thought I could beat any skylark with my melody, but now I might as well be an old crow bargin' over a potato field for all you seem to admire me. Do you remember the first time you heard me singin' that song? It was at Murty Dolan's weddin' where I laid eye on you for the first time, and you wearin' a blue dress with white buttons on it. You had a fringe down to your eyes and everytime you looked at me I thought of seein' two blue violets smilin' out of a clump of brown leaves that would be lyin' on the ground in April. I kept watchin' you while I sang that song and you blushin' like a rose and pretendin' not to notice that I meant it all for you. Afterwards I heard you sayin' to Rose Fagan that you never heard a grander voice comin' out of a man's head than my own, or a lovelier song than what I was after singin'. But I suppose that's too long ago now for you to be rememberin', and the old come-all-ye isn't good enough for you anymore. It would take the great John McCormack to be liftin' a stave of a song for you these times since you got set up with a gramophone, bedad."

Mrs. Fahy went over to her precious barmbrack and, cutting a wedge off it, laid it before her spouse as a peace offering. "Here Tom, put that in your mouth," she said, "it will sweeten your recollections. Well you know I'd rather be hearin' you croakin' around the house even with a cold in your head than any of them do be yellin' themselves hoarse on the gramophone. Sure I was only fearin' a blast of that cold wind would go down your throat and kill your grand voice entirely and be leavin' me without anything to cheer me up at all. Next time Galway Jack comes the two of you must have a real concert together and then I'll be in my element. Is the tea strong enough for you? I could see the bottom of your cup pourin' it out, and that's nothin' to be givin' a hard workin' man of a cold night."

Mrs. Fahy put another spoonful of tea in the teapot and spread out a coal of turf for further drawing for Tom's particular comfort.

"You know very well," she continued, "that I don't forget the night of Dolan's weddin' any more than yourself. Didn't I spot you out the very minute you came into the room and asked Tim Casey who you were! The young rascal told me you were the worst character in the parish, always in jail for poachin' or shootin' agents or some divilment like that; it was a wonder Murty Dolan asked you to his weddin'. Rose Fagan told me the truth afterwards, but anyway, I felt you were the boy for me even if I had to convert you."

Tom laughed as he tried another cup of the strengthened tea, "You converted me all right, Mary," he said, "but whisht, someone is comin' across the street, Shep is givin' great tongue out there."

"Bedad, he is, and a welcoming tongue," said Mrs. Fahy, "I wonder if it could be one of the neighbors!"

As the door opened a blast of cold wind swept in, nearly blowing out the lamp and sending a whirl of ashes over the hearth. "Why, if it isn't Galway Jack, himself," cried Tom Fahy and his wife together as they were greeted by a hearty "My

Christmas box on you," by the newcomer.

Galway Jack it was, sure enough, and he muffled up to the eyes in a fine overcoat that made him look, as Tom said, "like a shah of Persia." His beloved ash plant was under one arm and several packages were securely tucked under the other. Jack's face was beaming like a full moon with holiday festivity. He was soon ensconced by the fire with a cup of steaming tea beside him and a wedge of the barmbrack in his willing hand. The mysterious packages were laid aside to be opened after the ceremonies of hospitality had been properly observed by his hosts.

"I was thinkin' of you when I made this cake, Jack," said Mrs. Fahy as she sampled a piece of it herself, "I remembered the story that you told us of the time you spent a christmas with the minister's family up in the North when the old Cook put plaster of Paris instead of flour in her bakin', and you broke a tooth tryin' to get a bite out of the fruit cake she gave you. Do you remember the time you tried your hand at roastin' a turkey, Tom?"

Tom laughed and looked uncomfortable. "Sure it's about time you forgot that, Mary," he said. "You see, Jack, it was the Christmas after we were married, and I was a great one then to be helpin' about the house when I could, though herself there often felt like throwin' a pot at my head when I got in her way. But, havin' a sick cow to see after, I didn't wait for the late masses that Christmas morning, but hurried home leavin' Mary to get a seat back on one of the neighbor's cars. Everything was ready to be cooked for our dinner, includin' a fine young turkey that was plucked and all out in the barn. Thinkin', so long as I had a good fire down, I'd put it in the oven and surprise herself by havin' it well on the way to a grand brownin' when she came back, I started in on my cookin' job. There was I with a grand fire under and over my turkey and just sharpenin' the big carvin' knife when in comes Mary after gettin' a lift home with the Kellys. When she saw the oven goin' she gave a screech you'd hear a mile away and 'what have you in the oven?' says she. 'The turkey,' says I. With that she grabbed the lid off the oven and hauled up my poor bird that was just gettin' a nice coat of tan on him. 'I didn't clean him out,' she cried, 'All his insides are in him yet. O, murder,' she says, 'what will I do at all with our grand dinner gone to waste on us?' 'Hush up, woman,' says I, 'He isn't that far gone yet.' So I ripped up the turkey and washed him out before stuffin' him with bread and onions, and a grander tastin' bird you never ate in your life. So that was my last attempt as a chef and, to tell you the truth, I wasn't sorry to have my cookin' days ended. I suppose you'll be havin' a great set-out for Christmas over at the lodge."

Jack's face clouded, "No then," he said, "Mr. Barton and the missus are goin' up to Dublin for their holidays, and I must go to drive the car and help with the doin's in her father's place. They say there's goin' to be a great gatherin', so God knows what they'll be havin' me at whether I like it or not. Times are changed since my cattle drivin' days, Mr. Fahy."

"Well, I'd trust you to enjoy yourself wherever you are, Jack," said Mrs. Fahy, "but anyway, you can spend this evenin' here for we're dyin' to have a long chat with you, and Tom didn't hear a song or story worth listenin' to since you were here last."

Tea being over Jack opened up his packages, shyly saying he hoped they would excuse the liberty he took in bringing a few things in honor of the time that was in it. There was a brown silk scarf with a blue border for Mrs. Fahy, done up in tissue paper, and a grand briar pipe for Tom, a pair of tall wax candles the length of his own ash plant and six gramophone records of airs that he knew would get a warm welcome from both. There were loud outcries at Jack's gifts.

"Why, if that isn't the very scarf I saw in Galway last week," cried Mrs. Fahy. "It was in a big window and all my hints to Tom wouldn't make him get it for me. O, Jack, you must have paid a fistful of money for it!"

Tom Fahy handled his new pipe with a loving touch. "I shouldn't be takin' it from you, Jack," he said, "but I'll make a trade with you. There's that grand stick Dick Brophy brought me when he came home from America, and I want you to have it for my Christmas box."

Jack's eyes glistened, for the stick had always taken his fancy. With a stylish thing like that in his hand a fellow might land in all kinds of good luck. The exchange was made and happiness reigned.

"I wish we were havin' you here to be helpin' eat the fine puddin' I'm makin'," said Mrs. Fahy, "Last Christmas I kept the leg of a goose nearly a week thinkin' you'd be droppin' in to sample it. Tom said I should save you some of the goose grease to put on your heels after the Christmas fairs."

"If I had some of that same grease last year, Mrs. Fahy, it's on my tongue I'd be needin' it instead of my heels," laughed Jack, "I don't think I ever told you what happened to me in the city of Galway about this time, then."

"No indeed, you didn't say much about where you were or what you were at, Jack," said Tom Fahy, "but we both noticed you weren't yourself at all when you rolled in at New Year."

"It's queer the foolish things a man will do sometimes, and how one foolish thing will lead on to another," said Jack as he stared into the red heart of the turf fire. "Before I tell you about my last Christmas adventure I must go back to that time you were speakin' of when I was workin' for a minister up in the North. There were fewer years on me then, and I was as ready for a caper as anyone my age. After the poor old woman tryin' to put a rock-bottom foundation to our stomachs she was sent away bag and baggage, and a new cook hired in Belfast. In the meantime a young girl by the name of Norah Kane, whose brother was a gardener on a nearby estate, came over to look after the kitchen for a few days. Norah was from Connacht like myself, havin' come up with her mother and her brother from Leitrim to live in Captain Bell's gate lodge. I can't say what there was about that girl,

SHEILA
KERN

Mrs. Fahy, but a queer feelin' came over me the minute I laid sight on her."

"God bless us, Jack, did she have the evil eye?" asked Mrs. Fahy.

"Well she had two bewitchin' ones," answered Jack. "When I saw her by the door my heart turned over and I don't know if it ever got back in the same place since or not. She wasn't so purty to look at with her black hair and dark skin, but she had a way with her I never met in any girl before. I bid her the time of day and she answered back, but I felt her eyes borin' me through to my backbone, and I knew if she told me to walk on my head down the avenue I'd have to do it to please her.

"For the next few days I was like one in a dream, and I found more errands to be bringin' me around the kitchen than a cat to a dairy door. She never spoke much, but the two eyes of her would draw me through a knothole in a wooden plank. Then one day the new cook arrived from Belfast and Norah went back to the gate lodge two miles away, takin' all the light of day with her."

"Love is a terrible queer thing, sure enough," said Tom Fahy; "it makes a fool of the best man ever walked the earth, and well the women know that same."

"Well, I bit harder on it than the plaster of Paris cake," grinned Jack. "Anyway, all was left for me then was to try meetin' Norah at some of the houses where she used to go of an evenin' for a dance or a ceilidh. Like a big omadhaun I'd be leppin' around sets and no more dancin' in my feet than a plough horse, just because she'd be there fornint me with a comether in her eye. You may well laugh, Mrs. Fahy, but I couldn't help it."

"I'm not laughin', Jack," said Mrs. Fahy; "anyway, I'm not laughin' at you, but others who did the same," and she gave a look at her husband.

"One night when she didn't come down to Doherty's as usual I strolled up to the gate lodge on the hope of havin' a

chat all by ourselves. It was a fine evenin' with a new moon up
and the smell of frost on the air, a great evenin' to make your
feet travel fast when love was warm in your mind. As I was
passin' by a field near Kane's I spied a girl with a red shawl on
her head standin' by the gate and knew it to be Norah – for
I'd know that little red shawl anywhere. So up I goes and
stands beside her.

"What I said I'll never be tellin' you, but the words ran out
of me like a shower from the sky. I told her I was wild about
her and would never know a day's peace till she'd give me the
word I was dyin' to hear. Verses of old songs I recited to her
like I was another Raferty, and the sweat was standin' out on
my forehead for all the cool of the night air when I heard a
laugh behind me and there was Norah herself standin' on
the road pointin' to the one beside me, and says she, 'You'll
have to talk louder than that, Jack, before she hears you, for
that's my mother and she's stone deaf. Anyway she's not up
for marryin' this year,' says the young divil, 'so all your grand
language is gone to waste.'

"With that the old woman turned round and when she
saw who was tightenin' her up to the gate she treated me to
another string of talk that sent me skelpin' off home like a
pack of beagles was at my heels."

"And what happened after that?" asked Mrs. Fahy who
loved nothing better than romantic adventures.

"Enough happened then and after to send me hurryin'
back to Connacht," said Jack. "But sight or light of the girl I
never saw again till last Christmas, though many a time her
face was before my mind and I walkin' the length of the
roads."

"And you saw her last Christmas, Jack," prompted Tom
Fahy.

"Yes, I saw her last Christmas," said Jack wistfully. After
nigh twenty years I found her in the city of Galway havin'
heard by chance that she had married and gone there to live
soon after she left Ulster. Hearin', too, that she was a widow I
made up my mind to see if anything of the old Norah Kane

was left in her. And that's why I missed gettin' a leg of your goose, ma'am, or a taste of your plum puddin'."

"Well, I suppose you found her crabbed as her mother and maybe, as deaf, too," said Tom Fahy.

"No," answered Jack, "Of course the years had left their mark on Norah, but her eyes were just the same, and believe it or not, before I was ten minutes talkin' to her I felt the same queer feelin' all over me that I felt when I saw her first. That was Christmas Eve and that night I bought a grand card and put it into an envelope with five pounds I had in my pocket all ready to give to her for a present when I'd go to her place for dinner.

"The hours seemed years long till it came for me to set out for Norah's home next. With my mind runnin' on all I was goin' to say I wasn't too pleased to meet with big Ned Molloy at the corner of the street where she lived. He was a lad I used to know on the roads, a hard customer that I'd sooner steer clear of at the best of times. He kept step with me on the way and when we came to Norah's door, says he, 'I'm goin' in here to eat a good dinner with the woman I expect to marry next month.' When he said that I felt the street had given way under my feet. I looked at the big red face of him and couldn't speak for a minute.

"'Are you meanin' Mrs. Callaghan?' says I, 'Mrs. Norah Callaghan?'

"'Of course I'm meanin' her,' says he 'And how do you come to be knowin' her?'"

"'O,' says I, 'I used to know her up in the North when she was livin' there years ago. Well, Ned,' says I, 'Will you please tell her I'll be droppin' in some day in the week to wish her luck but I haven't time to be seein' her today.'

"'Sure I will Jack,' says he, 'but I don't think she'll be missin' you so long as I'm there to keep her company.'

"If I had that bit of goose grease to oil my tongue I might have said some things then I'd be sorry for now, Mrs. Fahy, but two days later I was on the roads again leavin' my five pounds in my bank where there's more to count beside them now. So you may say if I lost in one way I gained in another."

"So that was the last of Norah and her comether, I suppose, Jack," said Tom Fahy while his wife shook her head in sad disapproval of all the rest of her sex. "It is on my side," said Jack, "but I got a letter from her yesterday wishin' me a merry Christmas and tellin' me the terrible hard times she is havin' with the turk of a man she married. She wants to know when I'll be in Galway, and if I'll come to see her very soon."

"Don't tell me you're ever goin' within reach of that woman and her two eyes again, Jack," cried Mrs. Fahy as she started in working on her pudding again.

Jack shook his head. "It's a wise man who knows when he's beat at a game," said he, "and in the game of love it's generally the women have the winnin' cards. Poor Norah has a bad partner to deal with, but I'll let them play it out together."

"Musha, Jack," said Mrs. Fahy, "I was just sayin' to himself there this evenin' when he was singin' one of his old come-all-yes that it's a hymn we ought to be havin' so close to Christmas. Have you one yourself you'd be givin' us?"

"Sure, God help me, I'm short on hymns," answered Jack, "but if Mr. Fahy will bring the gramophone here to the table I'll be playin' you the grandest Christmas hymn was ever written. I brought the record of it sung by a great singer, entirely, and with real music to go with it." Tom Fahy carried the gramophone down from the little parlor and set it beside Jack on the kitchen table, and soon they were listening to the glorious strains of Adeste Fideles to an accompaniment on the violin by Kreisler. Such music had never rung through the humble home before, and even the boisterous winds outside seemed to hush themselves to be listening to it there.

Tears were in the eyes of all three hearers as they sat with bowed heads and clasped hands while the "Venite Adoremus" seemed to echo the songs of the angels heard over Bethlehem on the first holy Christmas night so long ago.

TERESA BRAYTON (1933)

The Ballymaconkey
Christmas Club

THE BALLYMACONKEY CHRISTMAS CLUB was unique, that is to say, it was not like other Christmas clubs; originally it had been started on philanthropic lines, and though it had moved a little with the times it still remained a club apart from others.

Everyone paid into the club what he could afford or what he wished, and everyone took the same chance in the draw, hence the poor member had an oppertunity of winning the Champion Christmas Hamper, and if the rich member came off with an inferior "draw" he could solace himself with the comforting reflection that his poorer brother had benefited materially and he himself spiritually by virtue of a deed of charity.

Everyone in Ballymaconkey supported the Christmas club and everyone approved it, everyone except Mr. Terence Mac-Grath.

Mr. MacGrath was the richest and the meanest man – some said in the village, others went further and said in all the country. There might be a doubt about his riches in this respect, there could be none about his unenviable character-istic, and it was that very characteristic that brought him into the Ballymaconkey Christmas Club – and – but we anticipate.

Little Seamas Mulligan came round to Mr. MacGrath's door with the tickets; little Seamas had come the year before and been shoo'd away, but he was a bold spirit and not easily daunted; moreover, his dad and two of his dad's cronies had promised him sixpence if he sold a ticket to Mr. MacGrath – so Seamas ventured.

To the small boy's intense astonishment he was successful, and that at the first essay. As a matter of fact Mr. MacGrath had been giving the matter some thought, he had seen the notices of the club posted in shop windows, and it had dawned upon him that if he could get a Christmas hamper for a few shillings it was worth it – so he gave Seamas two and sixpence and received in exchange a pink ticket.

The transaction was the talk of the "Blue Sheep" and the "Irish Wolf-hound" for days to come, and many earnest hopes and prayers were uttered that Mr. MacGrath might get his money's worth, and that only.

Everyone bought a ticket, even Patsy Reilly, father of an ever-growing family to whom a Christmas hamper was a wonderful treat; even old Miss Reilly at the other side of the village, that elderly spinster who was reported to live on air and the spiritual sustenance one is said to receive from performance of good deeds; small Seamas had his own ticket saved up for carefully, and even Father Murphy, fondly believing that his left hand was unaware of the actions of his right one, had exchanged one piece of paper for another.

The draw was arranged for early in Christmas week, it was an exciting event, as you may well imagine; the scheme was that everyone got something, even if it was only a cake or a fowl; but everyone cherished the hope that he or she might get the big hamper or one of the smaller ones – those wonderful hampers containing everything from tins of sardines to a bottle of the best whiskey.

The ticket holders and their friends congregated in the Ballymaconkey Recreation Hall on the appointed evening and waited anxiously while the club officials performed their mysterious rites. Presently Mr. Mulligan ascended a chair, holding a sheaf of papers in his hand.

"I will now call the numbers out," he announced, "and let each of you that hears his name called come forward and Denny here will give him what he's got – "

The audience held its breath.

"Number 5997783B!" read out Mr. Mulligan.

Mr. MacGrath stepped forward, he had won the big hamper.

Amid a strange and pregnant silence he walked up to the front of the room. Patsy Reilly tried not to catch his wife's eye, he knew she was thinking of the children; Father Murphy was guilty of a thought of the sundry poor families he might have visited on Christmas Eve; Miss Patricia Mary Reilly had a sudden vision of her very empty pantry, and another vision.

She had once been engaged to Terry MacGrath – no one in the village knew it, especially as she and Terry did not recognize each other now; nevertheless she had been engaged to him and had been fond of him, and then the widow Galligher had come along, the rich widow, and Terence MacGrath had changed his mind.

No one in Ballymaconkey knew about it. Miss Reilly was a kindly soul, everybody's friend in need, but at other times she was "standoffish" and kept her affairs to herself – she who would have given away her soul in charity was not likely to be connected, however remotely, with Terence MacGrath.

Meanwhile the winner of the Champion Christmas Hamper was tugging the same article home, he was doing so under difficulties, and the hue of his face was not entirely due to his physical exertions; the older people might be restrained by politeness, not so the younger.

"God bless us! Look what he gets for half a crown; he won't buy a bit of food for the next year."

"Sure it'll do him for the remaining Christmases of his life."

"'Twould be a charity if the tinned fish poisoned him."

These and other snatches of conversation reached Mr. MacGrath as he carried his prize home, and in spite of his reputation he did feel well – not quite as elated as he might have done as he opened his prize and examined its delectable contents.

He selected a tin of fish and opened the same for his supper, he made a hearty meal and presently went to bed.

Now having long past that turning point in life when man is meant to be either a fool or a physician, Mr. MacGrath, hav-

ing achieved the latter, took great care of himself and paid the most minute attention to his health, therefore physically, as well as mentally upset, he awoke from a night of terrible dreaming.

All night his wife had haunted him – she had brought him money but she had not brought him happiness; he had at first feared her, and by and by disliked her; she had never hidden her opinion as to his meanness, it was not long before she discovered why she had been married, and in death as in life she had rallied her husband on his fault.

"You're the meanest man on God's earth, Terence MacGrath," she had said to him a few days before her death, stung by his efforts to get her the cheapest of "nourishing food" ordered by the doctor, "and if I get the chance, every mean thing you do after I'm gone, I'll come back and haunt you, so I will – "

She did so in dreams that night anyway.

Mr. MacGrath felt very miserable all that day; although it was wet and cold he went out and dug the garden, anything to get away from his thoughts; thanks to a garrulous charwoman, he had all the village gossip; he knew how poor Patsy Reilly was, and how Father Murphy himself, a poor man, had scraped together that pound to help the club – thanks again to the same source, Mr. Terence MacGrath learned what Ballymaconkey was thinking about him.

"Sure they do be sayin' you're terrible mane," remarked Mrs. Leahy as she carried in the potatoes for dinner. She had no fear of man before her eyes, she was "cheap," and for that reason she knew her place with Mr. MacGrath was secure.

"I don't care what they say," said Mr. MacGrath defiantly.

"'Tis as well to have the good prayers of the poor," reflected Mrs. Leahy aloud. "I hope you'll be remembering it's Christmas, Mr. MacGrath," she added meaningly.

Mr. MacGrath dived into his pocket and threw her a two shilling piece, then having finished his meal he hurried back to the garden again.

He rather dreaded going to bed that night, but he forti-fied himself with a glass or two of the excellent whiskey in addition to a dainty fish supper – and retired.

He passed a night of horror – his wife was with him, she even tried to strangle him – he awoke in a sweat of terror – and although it was not yet dawn, he feared to sleep again.

He could not rid himself of the dreams and horrors of the night, he ate little breakfast, and went again to the garden where he pottered about till dinner-time.

At this point he met with a slight distraction. Mr. MacGrath was a veracious reader and his one extravagance was literature, especially that bearing on physical well being.

With real belief he seized on the bundle of papers which the post had brought him from Dublin.

Suddenly he rose from the table hot with a new fear, he had a paper in his hand, the glaring headlines shouted a new terror at him –

"DEATH IN THE TIN"

"It is now known that certain fatal bacilli lurk in tinned food, especially tinned fish," declared the paper. "They create a poison in the system which suddenly manifests itself, and after a few days or even hours of intense suffering, the victim meets the welcome release of death. The general sequence is as follows: The innocent victim partakes, perhaps, on several occasions of tinned fish; at first no ill effects are felt, then fol-low several nights of disturbed sleep, horrible dreams, loss of appetite, general depression; a day or two later the joints stiff-en, finally convulsions ensue, terminating in death – "

Horrible dreams, depression, loss of appetite – no stiffen-ing of the joints – yet, but that was to come. Mr. MacGrath sank down on a chair.

That cursed basket – he must get rid of it – he must pla-cate the Fates – wildly he thought, considered, then he performed the highest sacrifice of which he was capable – he took out his purse.

From this he extracted a pound note, this he placed in an envelope which he put into the paper, he packed the hamper for posting, and without even waiting to get a hat or overcoat, he dashed out into the rain.

As he lifted the hamper to be weighed by the postal officials, he was curtly reminded that he had forgotten to address it.

With trembling hands he seized a typical post office pen and hastily wrote the name and address of Mr. P. Reilly, then having seen the hamper out of his hands – that unlucky hamper – he went home wondering if he were doomed.

He spent the evening reading the piece of flamboyant journalism that had worked the spell, and watching for the first symptoms of stiffening joints.

Next day was Christmas Day, and Mr. MacGrath woke to the consciousness of a body encased in iron, he was stiff all over. And added to his physical suffering was his mental horror – the poison was at work – he was doomed.

Mrs. Leahy "might come in later," so the unfortunate man had to crawl out of bed and drag himself to the gas stove, where with great difficulty he managed to prepare a meal of sorts; he left the door unlatched, and then after many struggles succeeded in getting on some clothes. The lighting of a fire was impossible, at least for the moment, but he pulled a chair up to the still warm grate in the kitchen and sank into it, keeping an eye on the door in hopes someone might pass whom he might beg to get a doctor.

But no one passed the isolated cottage on Christmas Day and the hours rolled on.

It was really only midday but it felt like an age to Mr. MacGrath, when at last steps sounded outside – a womans steps – for once in her life Mrs. Leahy was welcome, her employer raised his head.

"Thank God you've come – I've been watching for you for

hours – I'm dying."

"Terry!" said a voice.

Miss Reilly left diffidence on the doorstep and came forward.

"Terry – did you mean to put a note in and forgot? Oh! What is it, my – my – dear."

He was conscious of nothing but his own plight.

"Get the doctor Patsy, will you – I'm very ill, I'm poisoned."

Without a word she disappeared as quickly as she had come, and within a remarkably short space of time she came back bringing a disgruntled medical man who was being disturbed in the very act of carving the turkey.

"What's wrong – too much good fare?" queried he unsympathetically.

Mr. McGrath pushed him over the paper.

"That's what I've got," he said in a feeble voice.

The doctor glanced at the page and then said one word: "Tosh!"

A few questions, a painful examination of the undoubtedly stiff joints, and the verdict:

"Acute indigestion from fish suppers, and rheumatism, you've been digging and getting wet. Ask this good lady to get you a solid meal – no meat – and light the fire. One guinea, please. I'll send over a bottle and give you a look in the morning."

And strange as it may sound, Mr. MacGrath laid down that guinea as a devotee lays his gift on an altar.

Half an hour afterwards when he had partaken of a meal and was warm and easy before a blazing fire, he ventured his thanks.

"Thank you for coming," he said, "If it wasn't poison, Patsy (unconsciously he had gone to the language of his youth), I was very bad."

"Thank you for your basket, Terry," she said; and although she was many a day advanced into the winter of her life, Terry MacGrath realized that the love of his youth was a comely woman. "They were talking against you in the village, but I always knew you had a good heart with all. What moved you to send it?"

There was a moment's silence, during which perhaps we may be bold enough to believe that the recording angel turned his back and put his fingers in his ears.

"Sure, I knew you wanted it worse than I did, Patsy," said Mr. Terence MacGrath, and he looked round at the room suddenly made homely by the touch of a woman – "I want a Christmas present from you."

"I haven't anything," she said doubtfully, for she half guessed.

"You've got yourself, and it's terribly lonely here," he said.

Through the color which was very becoming, though it did not suggest a Christmas rose, she agreed with him.

IVAN ADAIR (1922)

Percy's Christmas Party

❧

L OVE ME ONCE AGAIN."

John McCormack, through the medium of a much-scratched gramophone record, was entertaining an audience of one. Percy Percival, the owner of the said unmusical instrument of torture, listened enraptured to the famous Irish tenor's top notes. Then as a kind of running accompaniment, hummed "And another little drink wouldn't do us any harm," and proceeded to sample another John Jameson. From the foregoing my readers can guess Percy was some Johnnie.

He was a bachelor of 29 years, and occupied the two-pair front in a house on Mountjoy Square. Many match-making mammas had him earmarked, eligible, very eligible. His landlady, Mrs. MacGustie, had docketed him for Anastasia, her eldest unmarried, and if Percy was the recipient of many little dainties, that found no place in his weekly bill, he never gave any sign; he guessed the motive.

He rarely mixed with the other boarders. This aloofness made him rather unpopular with the males and much sought after by the ladies. They relished a hunt where the victim to be was elusive and not easily altared. If Percy preferred his gramophone and the seemingly necessary liquid refreshment, the reason was – bashfulness.

He never could be induced to join in any of the house parties or "hoolies" as the up-to-date flappers designate musical evenings.

Now when I tell you Percy was a civil servant you can immediately grasp the idea; he was a worker.

31

Like all such officials, he spelled work with a capital. He dreamed of it, and slept at it, therefore he was rewarded with rapid promotion, increased salary, and bonus.

Do you wonder, then, if all the girls in the neighborhood cast glad eyes at Percy each morning as he sauntered to Upper Merrion Street?

Percy's saunter was a thing not to be copied by any commoner; it was a hybrid between a fox-trot and the ostrich stride. A fortune awaits any enterprising producer who films this governmental poetry of motion. In fancy I can picture all the Dublin flappers, with their pigtails or bobby heads, gazing entranced at Percy on the screen, and their sighs thereat would probably lift the roof off the La Scala.

On this particular evening the subject of my story was in a very dull humor, and all John McCormack's records or John Jamesons' half-ones failed to rouse him. The cause was, Anastasia's mother had invited him to a Christmas party, and would take no refusal. "He must be more sociable, and the girls said they would use force, if necessary, but come he must." That was the ultimatum he was digesting, and he found it very tough. How could he look dignified hopping around playing "Kiss in the Ring" with a lot of giddy girls? Fancy playing "Postman's Knock," and being assigned to kiss some old geeser, with a face like a bath-bun, fourteen times. The very thought gave Percy the cold shivers. Then "Forfeits," "Vegetable Snap," "What is it like," and all the other idiotic ideas of fun. Percy was having a bad time communing on his coming ordeal. He meditated flight, then suicide, anything would be better than spending the evening with a lot of bobbed-haired dolls. After several little comforters from John Jameson, he realized there was no escape. Why should he be afraid; other fellows went to parties, why shouldn't he?

Arriving at this frame of mind, he began practicing. Putting the "Merry Widow Waltz" on the gramophone, he was soon pirouetting round the room. Not being used to violent exercises, his head got giddy. Of course it may have been the half-ones imbibed too frequently; anyhow, Percy bumped into a bamboo flower-stand with dire results. The plant, Anastasia's Aspisdistra, in an ornamental delph flower-pot, found a resting place on Percy's head, while that gentleman's neck was securely held by the bamboo stand. The carpet was profusely covered with the earth that kept the plant from an early decay. Anastasia was the first on the field, or rather, carpet, and I regret to state she laughed heartily at the scene before her. Holding a diploma for first aid, she soon disentangled Percy from the bamboo palisade, carefully removed the clay from his ears and hair and, with the help of her mother, who arrived with a rear-guard of four younger daughters, lifted him to a sofa. "Poor dear, he must have had a stroke. Matilda, run and bring me my castor oil"; so spoke the mother.

"Don't be silly, mother; what he really requires is a good glass of whiskey." This from Anastasia.

Proceeding to carry out her presription, Anastasia filled out a liberal dose of Jameson, which she insisted on Percy taking. Reluctantly Percy swallowed the potion and, addressing Mrs. MacGustie, said: "Your daughter, madam, missed her vocation; she is a most excellent doctor."

"Oh! Mr. Percival, you flatterer. I only hope you will be quite well for the party, as I want you to teach me your waltz step." Who says women have no sense of humor?

Once more alone, Percy examined his bumps and surveyed his features. Beyond a few scratches, which would soon heal by the aid of Gibsol, he was unmarked.

Proceeding to salve his wounds he discovered, too late, he had anointed his face with brown boot polish instead of the well–known Irish ointment. That night his dreams varied between dancing bamboo girls and jazzing bottles of castor-oil, but his opinion of Anastasia had gone up fifty per cent.

The evening of the party arrived. Percy was very nervous. He had dressed extra carefully. His tie was a beautiful shade of canary yellow; he looked perfect, and felt rotten. Bracing himself to face the ordeal of being introduced to goodness knows how many ladies of various ages, sizes and shapes, he prepared to descend to the drawing room. His idea was to proceed down step by step in a calm judicial manner, as a gentleman of his position should. What happened him he never could properly find out; probably his foot caught in a loose stair rod (such things do occur in boarding establishments). Anyway, Percy came down the stairs head foremost, and would most likely have sustained serious injuries if he had not landed on Mrs. MacGustie's sister, a lady of ample proportions, who at that moment was bringing in a tray containing an assortment of cups of tea and a plate of cakes. The lady had no other option but to squat down fairly and squarely on the floor.

Percy likewise squatted, after performing several acrobatic evolutions. Whereas the lady was minus her wind, Percy was full of tea and squashed sponge cakes.

When the lady recovered her speech, she told Percy several things, which I cannot print here, because the editor is a bit of a puritan, but you can take them as read.

It was fully ten minutes before Percy could get a chance to apologize, which he did most gracefully, and helped to assist the lady to her feet. This was a bad beginning for our friend, but being a government official he was not easily put out.

Mopping his tea–stained classic features, readjusting his canary–colored tie, which had now assumed the hue of a house-sparrow, he gallantly offered his arm to Anastasia, who arrived at this opportune moment, and they entered the room. His march past the assembled guests was a veritable triumph of deportment – bowing, smiling, handshaking, etc. He found himself safely anchored on a sofa in the darkest corner of the room, with Anastasia by his side. Feeling rather chilly, he made as if to seek some warmer corner.

Anastasia, with a look of alarm on her face, whispered: "Oh! Mr. Percival, I do believe you are sitting on the iced jellies."

It was too true. Percy could not see the extent of the damage done to his best Gordon Barclay holeproof, but he felt very cool towards Anastasia. Fortunately Mr. MacGustie appeared and took Percy into the inner room for a little refreshment. Producing a large bottle with a beautiful emerald green label profusely decorated with shamrocks and gold letters, he proclaimed it to be "Moore's Melodies Mellow Malt."

"Now Mr. Percival, say – when this is the real thing – Moore's Melodies – a regular 'Meeting of the Waters'" (three parts canal, and one part vartry – Editor).

Percy believed in a little whiskey if it was Irish, but he had a holy horror of Christmas fireworks.

He did all he knew to act "Pussyfoot" to Mr. MacGustie's "Mephisto." He talked music, eggs, art, politics, crops, Huckleberry Finnisms – anything to avoid Moore's Melodies, but MacGustie, who had had some, insisted on Percy drinking a Happy Christmas to everybody.

Percy, seeing that there was no escape, did so. From that moment he lost all sense of recollection.

Re-entering the room, where the guests were then engaged in pulling Christmas crackers, Percy made straight for Mrs. MacGustie's sister and, embracing her tenderly, planted a smacking kiss on that lady's nose.

She must have come from a football family. Her left foot met the fourth button of Percy's waistcoat. When they picked him out the fire-grate, he had developed two more bumps. Anastasia once more came to the rescue of her hero. It was remarkable the easy way his arm encircled her waist, and the sloppy look which he gazed into her eyes. Percy was evidently no amateur in some things. Music was now proposed. "Omaha," "Margie'" and many other music-hall classics were all duly murdered. Then Percy volunteered to sing some operatic selections. Don't blame Percy; Moore's Melodies was the culprit. The operatic solos consisted of "Paddy McGinty's Goat" and "Mick MacGilligan's Daughter, Maryann." Loud

ORIGINAL
MOORE'S
MELLOW
✦
MALT
MELODIES

applause greeted his sympathetic rendering of these beautiful ballads, and he retired once more to his sofa with eclat.

Games were introduced. Percy's shins were black and blue through falling over "musical chairs." He survived "Animal Grab," "Old Maid," and "Donkey," but lost 15s. at halfpenny Nap.

"Blind Man's Buff" was accountable for three more bumps, one on his nose and two on his forehead, but it was at "Consequences" he met his Waterloo. The fatal sheet of paper read out to all and sundry proclaiming: "The handsome Mr. Percival met the beautiful Miss M'Gustie in Mountjoy Square. He said to her, 'I love you.' She said to him, 'the feeling is mutual.' He gave her a ring, she gave him a kiss. The consequences were they were married and lived happy ever after."

Loud cheers greeted this. Percy was elated. Anastasia blushed becomingly. Percy, or "Moore's Melodies," whichever you will, rose gallantly and kissed her lovingly; she laid her hennaed golden-haired head on his manly shoulder, and sobbed joyfully.

Mrs. MacGustie beamed maternally on her favorite daughter, and wiped away a tear that wasn't there. Percy was quite unconscious of the sensation he had caused, and the innocent smile that adorned his features would have done credit to a child.

Most of the guests were now indulging in various dances, and the fun and enjoyment waxed merrily until the early hours of the morning.

●   ●   ●   ●   ●   ●

Percy awoke with a splitting headache. He had but the foggiest recollection of the previous evening's proceedings. A buzz-saw and several motors seemed to have taken up a temporary residence in his head. He paced the room in agony. Deciding to visit the nearest chemist, he carefully steered himself downstairs. In the hall he met Anastasia, who promptly embraced him. Percy's natural bashfulness reasserted itself.

He blushed (a lost art in Dublin) and disengaged himself from the fond embraces forced upon him.

The lady seemed mystified. "As we are to be married in January, Percy, you may kiss me. I will be ready soon to go with you to buy a ring, as arranged." Percy now had an idea – Anastasia was suffering from delusions. Mr. MacGustie, coming on the scene, looking anything but amiable, proceeded to give Percy a more or less faithful record of the previous night's happenings. Percy looked doubtfully at MacGustie's brawny arms, then at the hall door, bolted and barred; finally his gaze rested on the tearful Anastasia, who now played her trump card: she fainted. Percy caught her before she reached the ground – she saw to that.

Mr. MacGustie diplomatically withdrew. Well it's the same old story – since the Garden of Eden. Man is only in the halfpenny place when it comes to pitting his wits against a woman's. Poor Percy! I am a married man myself.

L. R. HENRY (1921)

The Compact

THE MOON CAME OUT from behind a bank of cloud, and for a few brief moments shed its soft light over the quiet countryside. Crystals gleamed in the snow, but the Christmas candles paled in the windows along the glen.

Paddy the Piper shrugged his shoulders, and gathered his old frieze cothamore closer around him. He had served a long apprenticeship to the road, and was familiar with its every mood. Night and day he had travelled it now for close on thirty years. Adversity drove him to it, and once caught in its subtle coils he had never been able to extricate himself. The dark clouds were travelling fast before the keen, cold wind. But nowhere was there a break in them.

The toot of a horn sounded behind him on the road, and turning round, he was almost dazzled by the powerful headlights of a motor. It approached noiselessly, and was upon him before he realized it. Then a voice called out:

"Hi, you! Is this the road to Caherboy?"

It was brusque and businesslike, the voice of a stranger who knew not the courtesies of the highway.

"Yes," answered Paddy, after a pause. "Keep straight on till you come to the cross, an' then take the road that goes to the left."

"How far is it from here?"

"'Tis a good two miles, an' a bit over, maybe."

"You going there yourself?"

At first the piper felt like resenting the man's curiosity, but as there was nothing offensive in the tone in which the question was asked, he decided to give the information required.

"Yes, I'm on my way there, sure enough."

"Right. Jump up beside me, and then I shan't have to ask my way again."

It was the first time in all his long experience of the road

39

that a motorist had offered him a lift. For a moment he wondered if he ought to accept. Would the offer have been made
if the man who made it had known that he was only a piper?

To set all doubts at rest he stepped in front of the car, and
stood in the full glare of the headlights.

"Here, that's not the way to get on, man," the driver shouted. "come to this side, and look sharp about it."

Mechanically the piper obeyed. After all, what did it matter what his calling was? At the entrance to the village he
could ask to be set down on the plea that his journey was at
an end. The car would resume its journey, and he would
never see it again.

As he stepped up beside the driver he caught a glimpse of
the gentleman who sat in state within. The occupant of the
car wore a heavy overcoat with a deep fur collar. He had huge
fur gloves, too, and a rug around his knees – all the appurte-
nances, in fact, of a wealthy man travelling for pleasure.

"You all right?" the driver enquired.

"Yes, I'm all right," Paddy replied.

The man nodded, and the car shot ahead noiselessly.
Never had the old piper travelled in such comfort before,
and never could he hope for a repetition of such an experience.

"Faith, they're great yokes," he confided to the driver as
they sped along. "There's no batin' 'em for gettin' about the
country."

The driver smiled inwardly, but otherwise took no notice.
At the cross-roads they turned to the left without slowing
down, and after a run of a few moments the piper laid his
hand on his companion's arm.

"Aisy now, like a good boy," he called out. "This is
Caherboy, an' if 'tis all the same to you I'll be gettin' out here.
Sure if the lads saw me goin' about in such a grand yoke as
this 'tis a holy show they'd make of me."

"But where's the hotel?" the driver enquired.

"Keep straight on till you come to the bridge," Paddy

directed, "an' 'tis the first house after that. There's two big lamps in the square in the front of it, so you can't make any mistake."

The man nodded, and Paddy alighted to discover that he had lost control over his limbs. But after a while the feeling wore off, and his old grip of the road returned. He played his first tune at the pump, and before long the pavements were lined with people. He was that "rara avis" among his class, a musician who was unaware of his skill. Moreover he was well known, and there were few in the village who had not a feeling of regard for him.

Air after air he played, "popping" the notes off the little leather strap fastened round his leg just above the knee. The airs were called from the pavement, and from the pavement came a shower of coins as each tune finished in a long-drawn wail. The holiday spirit was abroad, and the old piper's Christmas dinner was assured long before he was permitted to move on to his next pitch, higher up the road.

The owner of the motor in which Paddy had travelled to Caherboy was dining substantially, if not indeed sumptuously, in the commercial room of the village hotel, when the piper took up his stand on the other side of the bridge. His luggage was still in the hall, for the porter, who was also "boots," driver, and general factotum, had gone home to attend the ceremony of lighting the Christmas candle. Paddy played an old favorite of his own, "The Foxhunter's Jig," and as the rousing strains floated out on the crisp night air, the visitor laid down his knife and fork to listen. He was hungry, and had eaten with relish, but as the tune progressed, all thought of dinner receded. After a time he rose and opened wide the window, taking up his stand just inside, the better to hear the music. It was at that moment that the lanlord entered the commercial room.

"Everything to your liking, sir?" he enquired.

"Oh, yes," the visitor answered. "Everything's quite all right, thank you. Fine player, isn't he?"

"He is, indeed, sir, the finest in the counthry at present. There aren't many of 'em about now, an' more's the pity, for 'tis a grand ould insthrument. Still, ould Paddy is a host in himself."

"Paddy what?"

"Paddy the Piper, sir."

"Yes, but what's his name besides Paddy?"

"Oh, Molloy, sir. We think the world an' all of him, for he comes from this part o' the counthry, an' if 'twasn't for the 'meeah' he needn't be thrampin' the same as he is, poor man. He had as dacent a father an' mother as ever lived, but the bad times came to 'em, as they came to many a family around here. Wan by wan they sold every baste they had, an' in th' ind the farm itself wint to pay their debts. The father an' mother died soon afther. The two sons were fine pipers, no better, faith. Wan of 'em, 'twas said, got into a band in Dublin, an' saved enough money to pay his passage to America. He was th' eldest of the two, an' he took the pipes, though, I believe, 'twas the father's wish that Paddy should have 'em. What became of him in America I never heard. Paddy worked with several farmers around here, but after a time wint on the road. He was a bit wild, but as honest an' harmless a crayther as ever lived. When we saw him next he had a set of pipes of his own, an' I believe 'tis the same set he has still."

The visitor resumed his seat and passed his hand wearily over his brow. Outside the piper continued to play to ever increasing crowds.

When he moved on to his next pitch, and his pipes were no longer audible, the occupant of the commercial room rose from his chair, and stood with his back to the fire. The room was hung with holly and mistletoe, and the Christmas log was crackling in the spacious grate. The atmosphere of the room was pleasantly warm, but all the time he was conscious of the snow outside. Everywhere there was evidence of the Christmas season; but he stood apart, a solitary spectator, while in the streets outside, swept as they were by a biting wind, a good-humored crowd was following an itinerant piper, no less good-humored than they.

A feeling of utter loneliness came over him, and for a moment he almost envied the musician. But the mood soon wore off, and he went out to the door to see what the night was like. The clouds were still racing madly across the sky. The icy bitterness of the wind cut him like a whip. A stranger passing by bade him a merry Christmas, and in a dull unconscious way he returned the greeting.

Presently the landlord came out of the bar, and observing that the visitor's luggage was still in the hall, he made a clicking noise with his tongue against the roof of his mouth.

"That lad'll be the death of me," he remarked in a tone that bespoke his utter helplessness. "He's here, there, an' everywhere but where he's wanted."

The visitor turned round.

"Eh?" he enquired suddenly.

"Oh, it's that man o' mine I was complainin' of, sir," the landlord explained. When he was goin' out he said he wouldn't be long, an' here is your luggage still lyin' in the hall. I'll talk to him about this when he returns, my hand to you I will."

"It won't hurt there. It doesn't matter really. By the way, I'll have that case in here."

As he spoke, he picked up a long receptacle not altogether unlike a violin case, and entering the commercial room, dropped into a chair by the fire. The landlord returned to the bar and took out his ledger. He was engrossed in his accounts when the music of the pipes filtered into the shop and caused him to start.

"It can't be ould Paddy back again, surely," he thought. "But who else could it be?"

He bent over his ledger again, but the music distracted him. The player slipped easily from grave to gay in a fashion he had never known Paddy to adopt.

"The man's head is just burstin' with tunes," he remarked, "an' he's playin' to relieve his mind."

Closing his ledger, he put it away carefully, and went out into the hall expecting to find Paddy playing in the square in front of the hotel. But no, the music came from the commercial room, and already a little knot of people had collected in the road outside.

"Glory be to God!" he exclaimed, "'tis the visitor himself. Now who'd ever think that a fine gintleman like him would be able to play on a common insthrument?"

The town clock pealed the quarter chime, and with a shrug he knocked at the door.

"What time would you like dinner tomorrow, sir?" he enquired.

The visitor laid down the pipes at once.

"I shall not be in to dinner," he replied. "I'll be off about twelve, and will take some sandwiches with me."

The landlord nodded and withdrew. A step sounded on the square outside. It was the porter returning to his post.

"You don't mane to say you've come back, do you?" the master demanded. "Put up the shutters at once, an' thin take this luggage upstairs."

Next morning the visitor was up betimes, and after early Mass returned to the hotel to breakfast. He seemed much more sociable than he had been the night before, was surer of himself, and generally more at home.

"Well, I'm sorry you won't be here to dinner, sir," the landlord informed him after breakfast. "I have the loveliest ham an' the finest turkey that any man could wish to sit down to."

The stranger smiled agreeably.

"That I shall be unable to sample the good things you mention will be a source of regret to me during the day," he remarked. "But I am the victim of circumstances. However, I shall be back tonight, and cold ham and cold turkey – that is, of course, provided you can spare me some without inconve-

nience – will be very acceptable indeed."

Soon after he set out in his high-powered, richly-upholstered car, the landlord seeing him off from the door. When they came to a boreen some miles outside the town, the stranger alighted and bade the chauffeur wait.

At the end of the boreen were the ruins of what had once been a farmhouse. The walls were still standing, but there was neither roof nor window, nor door. The stranger with head bowed, and slow, faltering steps, passed in, and reverently uncovered. As he did so, he became conscious of the presence of another. It was Paddy the piper on his knees, with the beads of his Rosary slipping through his fingers. Instinctively he knelt down beside him, and for some moments there was neither sound nor movement. The floor had been swept clean, and the ruined walls sheltered them from the wind. The tattered frieze of the one was in marked contrast to the shapely broadcloth of the other, yet in that moment the pair had come very near each other, not in body only, but in spirit as well.

When they rose it was the stranger who held out his hand.

"You have kept the compact, Paddy," he remarked in a voice he found difficult to control.

"I've never missed a year, Shane," the piper told him.

"And I've missed God knows how many."

"But I always said you'd come back sooner or later, and I'm that glad this minute I could die aisy now."

The other glanced around the old place and sighed.

"We'll have it re-built at once, and spend the rest of our life together. 'Tis what they both would have wished, God rest their souls."

P. D. MURPHY (1919)

Christmas Roses

CHRISTMAS EVE! The rain was coming down in close sleety drifts, the wind was blowing it in the faces of the pedestrians, the streets were muddy and slippery, and the glaring lights were reflected in the wet pavements and pools of water. But neither drenching rain nor biting wind had power to keep folks indoors, and the streets were full of busy shoppers, hurrying along eager to complete their purchases and return to the cosy fire and warm welcome awaiting them. The shop windows flung down glaring squares of light on the pavements and displayed in all their brilliance the various goods suitable for Christmas presents. Anxious mothers stood debating the respective merits of woolly lambs and white monkeys, and wishing they could afford that most fascinating of Teddy Bears for the darling at home.

To Donald Power none of it was now, but all of it was interesting. He had returned to his native land after ten years abroad – years of strenuous, unremitting toil. And having grown rich and prosperous, he had yielded to an uncontrollable desire to spend Christmas once more in the old country that had ever been home to him, and had returned full of love and longing for his motherland. But, ah, ten years is a long, long time. Short enough sometimes when one is happy, and time, swift-winged and golden-footed, slips lightly by, but long enough when one is lonely without home ties or kith or kin. Time enough for many things to happen; for old faces to pass away and new ones to take their places; for old friendships to fade and old loves to die, if love that is true can ever die.

Donald had no kinsfolk in the old country, and but few old friends; and now as he paced the familiar streets, glancing around for the sight of some remembered face, he was conscious of feeling utterly alone and unwanted. All these people were intent on their own business; all of them had dear ones – mother, wife or child awaiting them. It seemed to him as if he were strangely out of place this Christmas Eve, since there was no one to care one whit for his going or coming. He had only arrived the previous night, and so far he had not looked up any of the few friends whom he hoped still to find; and already he half regretted the sudden unaccountable impulse which had brought him thither. He was almost sorry that he had yielded to the voice which had reached him out of the distance and called him home. Home! He had no real home. He was a stranger, an alien in his native land. A woman, shivering at the street corner, begged from him, a piteous look in her grey eyes as she strove to shield her baby from the merciless rain. He left her incredulous with delight, scarcely able to gasp out her thanks and blessings. She did not know that her eyes had reminded him of other eyes, grey, too – eyes which he had loved long since and lost awhile – eyes which had smiled on him in that far-off land of long ago. Where were they now, those sweet grey eyes? Whom else beside himself had they fooled? Had they led on the verge of madness? Well, he would never know. She had drifted out of his life ten years ago, and ten years is a long, long time. The old love-dream had long since been buried, but, ah! the grave was in his heart, far, far too close to be forgotten; and though the world knew not of its existence, yet he could not banish its memory, and sometimes the old sorrow stirred as if its sleep were not very deep after all. It was the shattering of that love-dream that sent him adrift on the waves of the world, hot with anger, sick with bitter pain, ten weary years ago.

It was a very commonplace story. He had been young, very young and impetuous in his wooing, and she had been the spoilt and petted only child of rich and over-indulgent parents. And when this masterful young wooer, whom in her heart of hearts she had crowned her king, laid siege to her heart, and would have taken her by storm, she had played with him a little to try her power. She had never meant to wound him, never meant to send him away, but she thought him just a trifle too high-handed. Where others had implored he had demanded, and she would fain have had him more humble, but his fierce young jealousy believed that she was only amusing herself, that she cared just as much for all her other suitors, and his bitter thoughts gave place to hot words between them, and each spoke words of high disdain. She had loved him, but she had been proud, and he had loved her, but was equally proud, and so while she had waited for his penitent submission he had gone away and left her, and never knew that she had broken her heart for him. That was ten years ago now, but no other woman had ever had the power to stir him, no other soft woman-eye had ever thrilled his heart as had those unforgotten eyes of shadowy grey. Had she only known it, that sweet love of his, she had triumphed in the end, for the place she had made for herself in his heart had never been filled, even for a time, by another.

He had been thinking of her all day, partly, he supposed, because it was Christmas time, and Christmas is ever a season for old memories to come haunting us. He remembered the last Christmas he had seen her. She had worn a white frock that evening, with Christmas roses in her hair and at her breast. He had mentally likened their snowy, stainless purity to her own fair soul, and had begged for one of the blossoms. He had it still, a crushed brown fragment, and only he could tell it was once a Christmas rose. He remembered how he had then called her by her name for the first time, Rosaleen, and had added daringly, "my Christmas rose!"

Since then the waxen flowers had always reminded him of her, and of the hopes which had been as short lived as the flowers themselves.

"Vi'lets, sir; vi'lets and Christmas roses," and a passing flower girl thrust her fragrant wares beneath his notice, "only twopence a bunch, sir – sweet vi'lets and Christmas roses."

They were smutted and drenched with rain, but still they were Christmas roses, and he bought a bunch and paid the girl six times their value, to her unbounded delight. As he left her his attention was directed to the brilliantly-lit porch of a picture theatre, where a gorgeously uniformed official kept guard. Outside a bill of contents promised a long and entertaining programme, while the imposing-looking official informed the passers-by that the performance had only just commenced, and that there were still a few seats left.

Feeling that he must pass the afternoon somehow, and that this was as good a way as any other, Donald turned in, paid his money at the little office, and passed through the door into the darkened room, where a picture was in process of exhibition. The building was fairly full, but there was an empty seat at the end of one row, which he took. He looked but with scant interest at the representation of a youth falling out of windows and down stairs, to the intense delight of the audience, if one might judge from their shrieks of laughter.

"Will you have a cup of tea?"

A voice beside him, a soft low voice startled him, for he had never heard but one voice with that low lilt in it, and he turned to see one of the pink-frocked, white capped attendants holding a little tray towards him.

"No, thank you," he said.

"Then, will you please pass the tray along?"

Again her voice arrested him, and he looked more closely at her. Her face was indistinct in the darkness, but its delicate oval, the heavy waves of dusk hair, all were familiar. It was a marvellous likeness, he thought, and then as the film was finished the lights went suddenly up, and in the glare he saw her plainly. It was no likeness, it was she, Rosaleen, the rose of his dreams; yet what a weary blossom she looked, with the old vivid radiance fled, a white, white rosebud now, and yet he would have known her anywhere. The sweet, grey eyes were sweet and starry as ever; the face as purely lovely as of yore, but the red lips drooped wearily, and the dark eyes held a shadow as if they had seen much pain. Yet she was still the same, older, sadder, wearier, it might be, but still the rose of all the world. But what was she doing here like this? What did it all mean? She, the petted child of fortune, here and in this dress?

"Thoughts from the tongue that slowly part,
Glance quick as lightning through the heart."

And all this passed through Donald's mind in that first brief moment.

"Rosaleen," he said, half involuntarily, and the girl started, and her dazed, frightened eyes met his in swift recognition. She had been pale before, but now she turned even whiter. From her very lips the color had fled. She looked as though she had seen a ghost, the ghost of her dead past.

"Rosaleen," he said again, and half rose, his eager gaze on her pale face, his eyes alight, heedless of the curious glances of those nearest to them.

"Hush!" she said, speaking with obvious difficulty, "please do not speak to me here; it is not allowed."

"Then afterwards, Rosaleen, I must see you, must speak to you – ." But she had passed on and left him with the pleading words still on his lips. The lights were out again and she passed out of his sight, but he promised himself that he would surely see her afterwards, would make her listen, would implore her to tell him all her story.

At the end of the next picture he looked eagerly around for her, but she was nowhere to be seen. He controlled his impatience, however, telling himself that as he had waited ten years he could wait till the close of the performance, when, he supposed, she would be at liberty to speak to him. On the stage a girl with a thin, but not unpleasing voice, was singing, and every word of her song found an echo in the man's lonely heart:

"Love comes back to his vacant dwelling,
The old, old love that we knew of yore;

He makes as though in our arms repelling,
He fain would lie as he lay before – "

In a seat before him a pair of youthful lovers sat close together, blissfully unconscious of any presence save each other's, finding the mediocre performance perfection, because they were near each other. Donald found it in his heart to envy them, for to them life was all rose and gold; for them it was the future, not the past, which held the completion of their love. They had not missed, even as he had done, the one thing, one, in his life's full scope.

At last the final picture was shown, and then the automatic piano gave forth the strains of the national anthem, and there was a general stir as everybody hurried away. Donald lingered, and was among the last to leave the place. He walked slowly up the passage between the rows of chairs, his keen eyes alert and on the watch for Rosaleen, but she was nowhere to be seen. The other attendants were standing about, but there was no sign of the one he sought. He went up to one girl, who was standing a little apart from the others.

"Can you tell me where the tall young lady is," he asked, "the one who brought tea down the left hand side of the center? I wish to speak to her."

"Oh, you mean Miss Molloy?" returned the girl, glancing with evident appreciation at Donald's bronzed good-looking face, and tall well-knit figure. If this were a friend of Miss Molloy's, she decided, he was certainly worth cultivating, and she would tell Miss Molloy so. "She's not very well, and she's had leave to go home."

Donald's face fell. His disappointment was very keen.

"Will she be here to-night?" he asked.

"Can't say, I'm sure. The boss told her she might stay away if she didn't feel better."

"Well, I'll come on chance," he replied.

"Can I take her any message from you?" asked the girl

kindly. She had a strong vein of sentiment in her composition. Anything in the nature of a love affair excited all her interest and sympathy, and she scented a romance after her own heart between this handsome stranger and her somewhat reserved friend. "I'll see her at tea time."

"You are a friend of hers?" he asked. She laughed.

"Yes, as much as the likes of me can be a friend to the likes of her. She's not one of us, Mr. – . You don't need to be told that. Miss Molloy's a real lady, and whatever has brought her to this job, anyone could see she wasn't born to it. She's proud too, and doesn't say much about herself, but she's so nice in her ways. It's there she shows she's a real lady, not a bit haughty or stuck up. She was real good to me, too, once when I was sick. I'll be only too glad to take a message."

Donald hesitated. The girl looked kind and dependable, yet what message could he send by her? Then a sudden inspiration came.

"Please give her these," he said, holding out the Christmas roses which he still carried, "with my love."

"I will," she said, heartily, and with that he had to be content.

Meanwhile Rosaleen Molloy, lying with her face hidden on the hard little bed in the "combined" room she called her own, was trying to force herself to calmness and to reason. That he, Donald, should have come back after all these years, that he should have found her in such a humiliating position; oh, it was too horrible! He was amply avenged now, she thought miserably. He had seen her pride brought very low. She felt that she could never face him again. She could not bear pity from him. How could she tell him all the sad story of the years since he had left her, of her parents' losses and ruin, of her father's suicide, and her mother's death from a broken heart? How could she tell him of that awful struggle when she had been cast literally penniless and sadly incompetent upon a none too merciful world, of her ineffectual attempts to obtain employment, of the utter failure of her

untrained services to compete successfully with trained workers, of her hopeless attempts at governessing, of her final des-
perate readiness to do anything – anything which would offer
her an honest livelihood? It was all so sordid, so miserable,
and when she had obtained her present post, through the
influence of a girl whom she had befriended when serving,
unsuccessfully, at a hat shop, she felt that she was too tired to
care what she did, that life was an unequal struggle for the
poor and the friendless, and that she would be very glad,
indeed, to lay its burden down. In a strange city – for her
home had been in the south – she had toiled and drudged
through the long years, and ever the thought of Donald, her
boy lover, shone through them like a ray of moonlight over a
dull sea, and now she had seen him yet once again, had
looked into his eyes, had heard him speak.

His look, his tones, had been kind, but, ah! she could not
bear his pity. She could not, would not see him again. If it
were necessary, she would seek employment elsewhere, but
she shuddered at the thought of once more renewing that
awful struggle. Then the door opened and her friend, Miss
Brown, came in, carrying a little bunch of Christmas roses.
Rosaleen's gaze rested on the flowers, for ever they spoke to
her – as to him – of the one and only love of her life.

"He said I was to give you these," said Miss Brown, "with
his love. That was what he said exactly, and, oh, what a lucky
girl you are. My dear, he's an angel!"

"Who?" asked Rosaleen, rather bewildered, but her color
came and went, as she took the waxen flowers. He had sent
them to her; then he had not forgotten, after all. "Why, that
gentleman who was speaking to you. You know right well. My
goodness, I only wish it was me he was sweet on," she concluded, with a half envious sigh, "not but that you deserve all
the luck you can get."

"I don't want to see him again," said Rosaleen, flushing.
"He knew me when I was in my happier days."

"And unless I make a great mistake he means to know you

again," returned the other. "Don't you be a fool, my dear. Love is the only thing that makes a woman's life, or a man's either, for the matter of that, worth living," which proved that Miss Brown, commonplace as she might be, had learned the meaning of life. "You'd better come tonight if you can. There'll be a crowd," she added carelessly, and then said mendaciously, "it's not likely he'll be there again so soon."

So it happened that as Rosaleen, tired and unhappy, left the theatre that night somebody – a very big somebody who had been patiently waiting for her outside – came up to her and slipped his arm through hers in the old masterful possessive way she remembered so well, and said gently:

"You are not going to send me away again, Rosaleen, are you, dear?"

And somehow she found herself telling him all the sad story of their lost years, and found it wonderfully sweet to rest her tired heart on his loving sympathy.

"Poor little girl," he said, when the pitiful little tale was told, and he pressed closer the slight arm he held. "We have made a big mistake, sweetheart, in thinking we could do without each other. I, at any rate, cannot do without you. There has never been a day of my life, I think, that I have not longed for you and wanted you. Oh Rose – rose of my heart, say you will give yourself to me now?" They had turned into the lonely street, where Rosaleen's poor lodging was, and there was no one in sight, and as she murmured her glad assent, he stooped his head and kissed her. "Mine at last," he said, "my Christmas rose!"

EVELYN CUTHBERT (1911)

McWhistler's
Mix Up
꧁꧂

I T WAS A MIX UP RIGHT ENOUGH. The ingredients were: Peter
McWhistler – small, nervous, and generally a teetotaller;
four and a half brace of assorted brats – only four of them
McWhistler's – the rest, cousins; several large female relatives
of Mrs. McWhistler's with attendant and insignificant hus-
bands; Mrs. McWhistler herself, who weighed twelve stone
twelve pounds on the penny-in-the-slot machine outside the
grocer's; and a Christmas pudding.

The latter work of culinary art had been perpetrated by
the eldest Miss McWhistler. This young lady was thirteen
years of age – a rather sinister number, by the way – and she
attended cookery classes in the college in the city.

Unfortunately on the day on which the plum pudding
was made, the lesson was on the preparing and cooking of
rabbits; and as the subject was rather depressing, Millie had
come home in rather bad form.

This made itself felt in the pudding which arrived on the
table on Christmas Day in very solid formation.

The McWhistler family always arranged to give its presents at the Christmas dinner. This year the juniors received
a collective gift of a huge Noah's Ark. Animals had been in
the air, so to speak, for some weeks owing to the competition
for young readers which had recently appeared in a certain
estimable magazine in which weird-looking shapes had to be
cut in two and distributed correctly so as to make normal animals from very abnormal-looking ones.

Peter McWhistler had heard a good deal about it, like
many other parents, and it had got on his nerves almost without his knowing it. The dinner was a success, although in its
later stages, the pudding weighed somewhat heavily upon

them. It was sweet and rich, if a little tough in texture and above proof in specific gravity.

Peter for once in a way had allowed whiskey upon his table, and this helped to lighten the gloom of the pudding.

Kindred spirits amongst the diners gravitated towards one another. After the meal and when the ladies left for the drawing room, and the children had adjourned to their own territory with their takings, the mere men opened another bottle and their hearts.

Peter planted himself beside "Uncle Charlie." I doubt if the juveniles could tell you his surname offhand, although he certainly had one. He was known to all as "Uncle Charlie" only. With infants he was jovial and genial; in the presence of grown-up females, he was suppressed; amongst men he was something of a cynic. Tonight, aided by the spirituous uplift of the whiskey, he spread himself a little more than usual. "Christmas comes but once a year, Charlie," said Peter, filling up his relative's glass. Peter had already had two small ones and was beginning to feel the devil of a fine fellow on that scanty provocation. "Let's be jolly." "Let's," responded Uncle Charlie, but not very enthusiastically. He had a harder head than Peter and it took more to thaw him. He swallowed his tot and Peter, as became a perfect host, went on with the thawing. "Well, how's things?" went on Peter, beaming on all and sundry. "Middling," said Uncle Charlie, "but they might be worse." "Come now, old man, you can't complain. Katherine is looking fine tonight." (Katherine was Mrs. Charlie.) "Yes, she's a fine gir – woman," assented her lesser half. He mopped his bald and glistening pate and his little eyes winked up at the corners with a smile. "A fine woman, but she's got a tongue."

"They all have," sympathized Peter. "When she gets going," continued the uncle, "about all these confounded old female pals of hers – well, thanks, just a little – it sickens me. All about their clothes and ribbons and corns and rheumatism – pah!"

"Well, we've got to make allowances, Charlie, got to make allowances. We can gossip a bit ourselves, you know."

"We talk – not gossip – sensible talk," said Charlie, banging the table with an argumentive fist. "Men never gossip. By the way, did you hear about Joe Queeze over there?"

Charlie jerked his thumb in the direction of a tall, thin man with a long red nose, who was industriously peeling a lemon.

"No!" said Peter. "What?"

The communication made in a low whisper, so as to avoid Mr. Queeze's ears, was evidently amusing, for Peter laughed – and didn't seem able to stop laughing.

"Ha, ha – to think that Joe Squeeze – ha, ha – not a bad one that. Well, well. At this time of life too. And can he do the fox-trot really?"

"He tried to, he looked like a camel," said Uncle Charlie. "You wouldn't catch me trying to dance. I'd look like a bear."

"No, Charlie, old chap, no; you – you'd not," asserted Peter in somewhat thick but very affectionate tones. "Camel– bear– no-no."

Peter's mind was drifting on a stream of punch towards the Noah's Ark and the competition.

"Did it ever strike you how like animals people are?" asked Charlie, who was becoming solemn and assertive.

"Joe a giraffe – myself a bear; Tim a monkey, Sam – a pig."

"Ha, ha! Yes, I see," said Peter nodding. "And what about the ladies? Are they like animals, too?"

"Certainly, Peter. My old woman – a cat. Your old woman– you'll excuse me, Peter?"

Peter nodded; he was in a mood to excuse anything.

" – Like a fat rabbit. Mrs. Tim like a snake – and – and so on. And then," went on Uncle Charlie, waving a hand impressively, "they're like things, too – Mrs. Mellix is like a plum pudding – the plum pudding we had tonight – too sweet to be wholesome – and – there you are. Hi! Where are you," for Peter had disappeared.

Poor Peter's "there you are" was on the floor to which he had slipped gracefully into oblivion.

Uncle Charlie was quite capable still. He rose from his seat and looked pityingly down at the smiling and unconscious Peter.

The other gentlemen hearing the cop had risen to render first aid.

"Poor Peter!" soliloquized Uncle Charlie, "He can't stand much. If he smells a cork it knocks him over. We had better get him quietly to bed, boys."

The "boys" agreed, and their host was removed gently but firmly to his sleeping quarters. The process roused him a little.

"Where – what – " he began in sleepy tones.

"It's all right, Peter," soothed Uncle Charlie.

"The animals," murmured Mr. McWhistler, "and the plum pudding – you said – "

"It's all right I tell you," repeated his comforter. "You and the animals and the plum pudding can all go to sleep together."

Charlie winked as they deposited the Usually-a-Teetotaller on his bed.

There they left him and went downstairs again to make whatever peace they could with the ladies by the aid of a few white lies.

But when Peter was placed on his bed he did not, according to his belief, stay there. The bed was soft, too soft, for it opened in the middle and he sank down right through it untill he came to a curious plain, covered with bright brown grass like the thin strips of paper used as padding in chocolate boxes. Peter had seen quite a lot of this material during the day. Just in front of him towered a huge wooden erection with red roof and pink sides, obviously a Noah's Ark. Peter was interested but not surprised. One is never surprised in a dream.

From the door in the Ark a figure advanced towards him.

Its head was bald, its eyes small and twinkling, with queer little gathered wrinkles in the corners, and its body was rotund. It looked exactly like Uncle Charlie, but Peter knew at once it was Noah.

"Good morning, Peter," said the Patriarch. "Are you looking for anything?"

"I don't know, sir," stammered Peter. "Charlie told me that I'd see the animals and the plum pudding when I – "

"Animals!" said Noah brightly. "You've come to the right shop for animals. I'm not so sure about the plum pudding. I must ask my wife about it. That's her department. Katty. Hi, come here. A gentleman wants some of your plum pudding."

"No, no," cried Peter hastily. "I don't want any, really – " even in his dream he had recollections of Millie's effort – "Please don't disturb the old Kat."

The words slipped out before he was aware of it and he looked in terror at the Patriarch, who might be able to make things unpleasant if he chose, but Noah only nodded and smiled.

"I see you have met Mrs. Noah before," he said. "Well, between you and me, I think you are wise not to risk that pudding – It's all right, Katty, you needn't come, the gentleman doesn't want any," he called over his shoulder. "Now," he continued, confidentially, "you see the pudding mightn't be what you would like. It's made of lots of things, including lead and glue." Peter remembered that he had thought of these two articles when sampling Millie's production. "Thank you very much," murmured Peter.

"Now," went on Noah, waving his hand in the manner of Uncle Charlie, "you were talking about animals. We'll go in and see them. I've had such a job getting them into the ark without breaking their legs that I don't want to risk tumbling them out again on the floor."

Noah put his arm round Peter's shoulder and pointed to the opening with a long staff. The funny thing about the staff was that as soon as Peter looked at it, it changed into a bottle of whiskey. Of course it didn't strike Peter as an unnatural thing at all.

They walked slowly up the slope towards the door. The clay seemed to cling to their feet, but this was scarcely to be wondered at as it was made of plum pudding – obviously poor Millie's.

At last, after toiling for what seemed like a long time, they reached the door.

Peter looked through it and saw a most extraordinary sight. There was a huge table with a Christmas tree upon it – the ark had conveniently disappeared – and around it were grouped animals such as never were seen outside a certain pictorial competition. In fact they were stranger still. There was a giraffe with Joe Queeze's long neck and thin face. A fat rabbit of enormous dimensions with a face like Mrs. Peter – an equally fat cat with a face like Mrs. Charlie. There was a snake, a fox, a bear, a lion, an elephant, and a hen, all with the heads of some or other of Peter's friends.

"Now," said Noah, "what do you think of that ?"

"They're very nice indeed," replied Peter politely.

"H'm, d'you think so? I'm not so sure. You see, they aren't quite right as they are. The children have to alter them to make them right and win the competition. I must call the children. Shem, Ham and Japhet – come here."

From somewhere a swarm of children rushed forward, each armed with a huge scissors. Their faces were the faces of the four and half brace of assorted brats mentioned before.

"What are they going to do?" asked Peter, backing away.

"Wait and see," said Noah, "and don't ask any questions. Men never gossip."

One child seized one of the composite animals and one another, and with one snip cut them in two. The severed people did not seem to mind in the least.

Why should they, for they had just turned into cardboard!

"Now," said Noah, "they've got to put the right pieces together and there you are."

At this moment, the top half of one of the "animals" began to object.

"Charlie," she cried; "Charlie, come here and don't be an idiot. Look what they've done to me, and there you stand like a fool, looking on and doing nothing."

Peter turned towards Noah, and saw at once, although he had altered very little, that Noah was gone and Uncle Charlie stood in his place.

"There you are," said Charlie, with a shrug of his shoulders. "The moment these women get into a mess they squeal for us. We're the worst in the world when everything is right with them. I think I'll let her stay where she is for a bit. She can't get at me anyway as she's cut in two."

"Can't I?" squealed his wife. "Can't I?"

How it happened Peter did not quite know, but it seemed as if Shem had stuck the correct halves of Mrs. Charlie together, for she advanced towards him quite her normal self, bad temper and all.

"Now you little rat, I'll teach you," she cried.

Once more Peter looked at where Uncle Charlie's head should be, but was not. At his feet crouched a trembling rat with Uncle Charlie's bald head on its shoulders. It looked up pitifully at him and squeaked.

"Please, Katherine," began Peter, the peacemaker, "don't be hard on him, he really didn't mean – "

"Fiddlesticks," cried the irate lady. "You whipper-snappers are always trying to back one another up. I'll teach you how to treat your wife."

Peter noticed that it was now his own wife and not Katherine who was advancing menacingly towards him.

"Children," she cried, "look at him. You forgot to cut that little monkey in two."

Peter glanced down and saw that he had the hind legs and tail of a monkey. The four and half brace rushed towards him, the hungry blades of their scissors clashing together.

"Cut him in eight, cut him in eight," cried Mrs.

McWhistler. "Eight! Eight! Eight!"

Nearer and nearer came the children and the scissors. They rolled him over and over and the blades came nearer and nearer.

"Eight! Eight! Eight!"

Peter opened his eyes and looked up. His wife was standing over him.

"Are you ever going to get up?" she demanded. "I've been telling you it is eight o'clock for the last ten minutes and you only jumped and grunted."

Peter sat up in bed. "If you had my dreams you'd jump and grunt too," he said, recognizing that he had just escaped from a nightmare.

"You disgusting little rat," said Mrs. McWhistler. "You were drunk last night, and Charlie said it was indigestion from poor dear Millie's lovely plum cake."

"Did you try any of it yourself?" asked Peter.

"Of course not. You know I can't touch rich things."

"Well then that's your luck!" grumbled Peter. "It was only indigestion really."

"You were disgracefully drunk – and whiskey twelve shillings and sixpence a pint, too – disgraceful."

"It was the plum – "

"Whiskey," interrupted Mrs. McWhistler.

"All right – plum whiskey – if that will satisfy you. What day is it, my dear?"

"St. Stephen's Day, and you've got to get up and do those things you promised to do when you had a free day. You've to paint and putty the greenhouse, and put a roof on the summerhouse, and mend the door and make that shelf for the pantry and mend the hole in the floor and put a cover on the armchair. Every man that's a man at all does a little work about the house on a holiday. Oh yes, and you've to dig the three beds in the garden and put in the manure. The plants should be in before now, and you know it. You had better do that first while there is good light."

Peter rose with a sigh. "Very well, my dear."
A very tired man went to his office on December 27th.

L. A. FINN(1925)

Barney Broderick's
Close Shave

꧁

I T WAS CHRISTMAS EVE. You could not be on the high road
from Knockkilcroghery to the market town of Ballyfin on
this particular day and be ignorant of the fact. For a
large number of vehicles, mostly donkey carts, drawn by all
sorts of eccentric and erratic animals, were coming from and
going towards the town, those returning of course being
laden with boxes and parcels of eatables and drinkables (the
latter including fairly large measures of "John Jameson" or
"D.W.D.," for in those days the house that would be without
"a drop of the cratur" at Christmas was either a deserted one
or non-existent). And, by the same token, the unfortunate
pedestrian who might happen to be on that road on this day
would want either a pair of eyes in the back of his head, or a
drawing-room mirror in front, to dodge the unusually con-
gested traffic of the Ballyfin highway. Sure, didn't poor
Paddy Magee, whose sight was none too good, get jammed
between two Spanish asses coming from opposite directions,
simply because he tried to look both ways at the same time.
And Murty Brady, the rather corpulent knight of the awl from
Carriganore, who was leisurely returning with some
"theeveens" and leather for Peggy Mackey's dilapidated
shoes, and whose eyes were glued on the ground, instead of
being directed straight ahead, or screwed around to act as
periscopes, wasn't he knocked down by a runaway
quadruped, followed by a jingling empty car, whose wheels
only struck the ground now and again.

But like Johnny Doolan's donkey, I'm afraid I've runaway
– from the chief episode of my rather rambling tale. Like the
majority of his neighbors, Barney Broderick, the local character, who was possessed of only one hand and one organ of

vision, wended his way to the town to bring home his Christmas supplies. He did not get knocked down by any "runaways" – catch Barney to be found napping so early in the day – for although his "lookout" was composed of the one and only orb which glistened beneath the shaggy eyebrow on the right side of his forehead – that organ was as useful to him as two were to the ordinary individual. Having reached the busy and bustling street in safety, Barney proceeded to make his purchases, and of course inevitably came in contact with many of his hospitably and humor-loving neighbors. Barney was, I needn't tell you, rather fond of "a drop," but he could manage to empty a good many pints down the mysterious depths of his capacious stomach, and start off walking afterwards as straight as a policeman, as if he had only just disposed of so much buttermilk or water. Indeed, folk that knew him (and where was the man, woman or child, within a twenty-mile radius, that didn't?) often wondered that he was not walking on his head instead of on his feet, and describing irregular curves from one ditch to the other, on his way home after a day's "booze." The only occasion on which he came to the barracks was when he stumbled up against a stray goat who was enjoying a feast of white-thorns on the side of the road. Suddenly imagining himself transformed from plain Barney Broderick to a full-blown Peeler, he seized the unfortunate goat by the horns and dragged her, much against her will, right up to the barrack gates, and into the mighty presence of Sergeant Sweeney himself. The latter did his best to look serious, but in spite of his efforts he burst out laughing at the comical situation, and brought all the available constables, who thought that the sergeant had suddenly had a fit, or gone mad, rushing into the room. But Barney, suddenly regaining his senses, in presence of the Force, dashed out of the room, leaving the Peelers to look after the goat.

As I said, Barney met many of his neighbors that evening; round after round of drink followed – Barney's measures disappearing before the others had lifted their glasses to their

lips. This continued until near nightfall, when Barney, who by the time was a fit inmate for one of the idle cells of the local "Black Hole," managed to get out of the town without coming in collision with any of the lynx-eyed officers of the law. He was the last to leave the town, and nobody, not even the writer, knows what time he arrived home that night.

It was close to midnight when Betty Broderick, Barney's elderly maiden sister, who was becoming anxious about the prolonged absence of her darling brother from home, opened the kitchen door and went into the yard to see if there was any sign of Barney's footsteps approaching. "It's time for any decent human being to be in his bed," thought she, as she shivered in the chilly night air, not of course suspecting that Barney was in his "bed" – of straw. Suddenly looking towards the barn on one side of the yard, she uttered a cry, and stood riveted to the ground by the sight which met her gaze. For from the spy-hole in the wall a long trail of smoke emerged, followed by others in quick succession, until the woman had no doubt that something in the interior was on fire. Her first impulse was to cry out at the top of her voice (not a very strong one at this stage of her life) in order to attract some neighbors who lived next door. Then she rushed for the largest water-pail in the house, tripping in her haste over tubs and "keelers" and other domestic utensils, dashed for the draw-well in the far corner of the yard, and ran with a pailful of water to the burning house. The door was only closed, so she rushed in, took in at a glance the situation of the fire, which was confined to a large heap of straw in the middle of the floor, and threw the contents of the pail on it. By the time help had arrived, and after several buckets of liquid had been emptied on the blazing mass, the fire was extinguished. Then, to the amazement and consternation of Betty and her neighbors, a form, not too unlike old Nick himself, arose from the straw. Betty, extremely superstitious, almost fainted at the sight of what she thought was the "ould boy," but who was in reality her own brother, who had fallen asleep on his improvised bunk, leaving a lighted butt of a candle beside his bed, and who had awakened with a state to find himself enveloped in flames (which graphically reminded him of the hotter nether regions). Barney was a sorry sight as he stood on the floor before his dumb-founded neighbors. His whole beard was singed to the roots, his face black and sooty, his tattered clothes dripping from the lately applied touch of cold water. It was indeed "a close shave" for him, but it taught him a lesson which he never forgot. And as he opened his prayer-book next day at the verse, "Abstain from strong drink or thou shalt perish therin," and this advice reminded him forcibly of a recent danger in which he was very near perishing.

From that day to this Barney shunned the "sparkling glass" as he would a cobra or an alligator, and he faithfully kept the pledge which Father Tim administered to him on that memorable Christmas Day.

SEAN MACELVOY(1919)

The Christmas
Raffle
_{ᖇᖇᖇ}

C HRISTMAS WAS A TIME of great merry-making in our village about thirty years ago when I was a youngster. We
had left the worries of school behind us and there was
all the fun of collecting the holly, roaming far and wide in
search of the berried kind. We were too young to give any
heed to the talk of our elders who seemed never to tire of saying that "things aren't what they were when I was a lad."
There were two concerts that took place in our village hall
and the raffles we helped to organize, going from door to
door selling the tickets and vying with one another in meth-
ods of salesmanship.

I remember well the year when Nick-the-Goat won a bottle of whiskey in the Christmas raffle. It was no use to him, for
it was his proud boast that he never touched a drop of intox-
icating liquor in his life. When the bottle of whiskey was delivered to him he set it up on a shelf above his turf fire, and at
every opportunity he would point to it and say to us, "Do you
see that bottle up there? Well the devil himself is in it, horns,
tail, and all!"

Of course, one or two of us knew that the liquor in the
bottle was not liquor at all, but we held our tongues and
winked at one another. When Nick had drawn the winning
ticket one of the bright boyos had said, "And what good is the
glory of it to the like of him? Wouldn't it be a shame to waste
it upon a man who's no better than a savage?" There and
then the bottle was opened and the lads drank to the health
of everyone around them. In the end they filled the bottle
again with water colored with brown sugar, and Nick-the-Goat
was none the wiser.

When Nick began to grieve about Puck, his goat, he

brooded for the first time in real earnest on the solace of the hard stuff. He would stare at the bottle on the shelf and say, "And do you tell me now that a man can drown his sorrows in the like of it?"

Puck was a sore trial to him. For months before Christmas, when ever we set eyes on old Nick, he looked a bewildered man. "It's Puck," he told us. "He has the life badgered out of me!"

Puck was the oldest he-goat in our parish and it lived in a little field behind Nick's cottage. It had one long pointed horn and a stub of where the other had been snapped off years before. It was so wicked that even the bravest of us was afraid to go near it, but Nick cherished it and not a word would he have said against it.

In winter the goat lived in a shed beside Nick's cottage, and when the weather grew really cold it rattled the door of the shed and butted at the wooden walls. This went on hour after hour with terrible relentlessness until old Nick was nearly demented.There was nothing for it but to bring the goat into the kitchen for a warm.

It was around about August when Puck got completely out of hand as if it had thrown all discretion to the winds at last. That was a fine summer and perhaps the heat made it long for the freedom beyond the little field. It developed the habit of spying on old Nick. It would peer over the ditch at him, watching until he went up the road to our village. Then it would set to work on the hedge that shut off the field from a boreen beyond and eat its way through the roughest branches.

There was nothing stopping it, and old Nick was tearing with anger because of its antics. In the end people began to complain that it was frightening even the children in the village. There were threats of shooting it, so that Nick had to tie it to a stake in the field.

This was a great blow to Nick and he sat in his cottage, brooding, staring up at the bottle on the shelf, as if he had betrayed his best friend. In early September a storm had broken over the village. Nick was dithering in fear like a hen that senses the presence of a fox. He was afraid of the thunder, and the lightning seemed to sear into his soul. He kept on looking at the bottle of liquor on the shelf, then he would rush out and shout over the ditch of his field, "Are you all right, Puck?" and then he would dash back through the rain to stare at the bottle again.

This went on until at last, in a fit of desperation, his hand reached up for the bottle.

In a jiffy the cork was out, and almost before he knew what was happening, the liquid was glugging down his throat. He sat, trembling with anticipation, waiting for the false happiness to steal over him. Nothing happened, and the storm went raging outside. He sprang to his feet when the storm was over and shouted out, "Lies! Lies! Ever since I was a brat in petticoats they've been telling me lies!" He rushed up the road to the village and dived into the pub. "Look at me!" he shouted out. "I'm a man with a head harder than the hardest whiskey in the land!"

When he left the pub night had come and the road down to his cottage was shrouded in blackness. He kept singing at the top of his voice, breaking off only to abuse his left foot for going one way and his right foot for going another way, and thinking all the time that the dark world around him was a strange and enchanting place.

When he reached his cottage the happiness fell away from him like a garment whisked off his shoulders by an unseen hand. He stood still, and his heart seemed to freeze. He felt his scalp pricking in the sudden terror. Two glaring spots were staring at him out of the darkness. He put out one hand gropingly and the palm rested on the point of a horn. "It's the Old Boy himself!" he screamed. "He's come for me!" He can never remember how he ran so far on that night, but when he woke in the morning he was lying in a field about a mile from his cottage. He was stiff and sore, and he knew then that he was in for a spot of rheumatics. Like a stricken man he trudged back to his cottage. He saw Puck squatting outside the door with the stake trailing from the rope around the old goat's neck.

The stake had lifted easily enough from the sodden ground and Puck was back at his tricks again, waiting impatiently for a warm before the fire.

The next day Nick handed Puck over to us."Take him away!" he said, "Do what you like with him! But I never want to set eyes on him again."

We kept the old goat in a haggard until Christmas and then we decided to raffle him. It was to be a surprise raffle. No one was to know the prize until the winner was declared, and we had no difficulty in selling the tickets because people had the itch of curiosity in them.

We drew the names out of a hat two days before Christmas, and believe it or not, the first name out of the hat was Nick-the-Goat! On Christmas Eve we took the goat down to his cottage in triumph. "He's yours," we said to old Nick, "You won him in the raffle!"

To the day of his death old Nick swore we had arranged the whole thing. He refused to listen to our protestations of innocence. All the same I believe that he was happy enough at the result. I can remember him now in the old days after that Christmas, with Puck squatting on the floor before the fire and old Nick smoking his pipe in the corner. There was a look of peace in his eyes, and some went so far as to say that they used to gossip to one another like two old men once our backs were turned.

REARDON CONNOR (1949)

One Christmas
Eve

⚜

1

I T WAS CHRISTMAS EVE. A real old-fashioned Christmas Eve. There was plenty of snow everywhere. The keen frosty air gave promise of it lasting. Out in the open country it lay in one pure sheet of white. The hoar frost glistened on the twigs in the hedges and sparkled on the branches of the gaunt and leafless trees. It glittered like powdered diamond dust in the red light of the setting sun.

Now and then the cold wind passing over the wayside trees shook from their snow-clad boughs little clouds of white flakes which added to the drifts that lay beneath them. The very sky was grey and heavy with more white down for winter's mantle, save in the west, and there in long lines of crimson and gold, the clouds awaited the setting sun.

"How beautiful nature is in its snowy robes but oh, how cold!"

So thought one lonely human figure who trudged along the country road that led to the distant town for which he was bound. He was an old man, very poorly clad in tattered clothes, and very weary, as one might see from the way in which he leaned heavily on his stick as he toiled slowly on.

With his long white beard, his silvery hair, and his rosy face, he might have passed as a ragged edition of Father Christmas, minus his sack of good things. But no Father Christmas ever yet gazed on this world with such sad and wistful eyes as did the poor wanderer.

Old, homeless, hungry and destitute, he tramped along his weary way. Milestone after milestone covered in frost he passed, 'til at length he came to the iron gates of a noble mansion standing in its own grounds. These gates were wide open, and the marks of many carriage wheels were on the snow.

"Christmas visitors," said the old man, as he paused and gazed at the marks. "Friends and relations coming from all parts to spend the happy season in the country. Food, warmth and wealth were all in there. Surely the owner of this mansion will not refuse a wayworn man a meal and a shelter for the night in some loft or barn."

Very timidly and humbly he passed through the gates and went up the snowy drive, bordered by gaunt and leafless trees from whose twigs and branches, outlined in silver frost, the little robins sang their winter song to the leaden sky.

My lady of the Manor sat in her boudoir which faced the drive. She was very much annoyed, and in the privacy of her own apartment she allowed her lovely aristocratic face to show it.

Only ten minutes ago she had intended to drive into town to complete her Christmas shopping and meet an old friend at the railway station who was coming to spend Christmas with her. Just as she was about to go out the news was brought to her that one of her famous pair of grey horses – the pair which she had so desired to show her guest, who was an ardent admirer of good horses – had strained a tendon in his leg and could not be used. She must now content herself with a brown pair of carriage horses. It was most annoying. The greys were the pride of her heart. The brown pair were nothing in comparison with them. No doubt but some carelessness on the part of the groom had caused the mishap. Stupid horrid man! He would be discharged after Christmas, and that was one comfort. A small thing to put her ladyship out of temper, you will say, my reader. But then, it never did take much to rise the ire of this pampered favorite of fortune, as all her household knew, from her husband down to the scullery maid. As she sat there impatiently waiting for the carriage to come round, her angry eyes caught sight of the old

man toiling up the drive. Verily he had come at an unlucky moment, for as a rule her ladyship liked to be considered charitable, and would bestow alms on anyone that asked for them, but now – here was a new grievance! She rang her bell imperiously. A powdered footman, whom nothing but his lady's "tantrums" could hurry, came quickly in answer to her summons.

"Look!" she exclaimed, waving her hand towards the window. "There is a dirty old tramp coming up the drive. I wager anything that the lodge-keeper has left the gates open. I shall let him know my mind presently. Turn that begging vagabond away at once."

"Yes, my lady."

He disappeared, and her ladyship, much ruffled, sank back in her well-cushioned chair with an angry flush on her face, and prepared a scolding for the careless lodge-keeper, thinking herself meanwhile – she who had scarcely a desire which was not granted, she, who on this Christmas Eve was rich, beloved and in the best of health – most unfortunate and ill-served. And wherefore? Because the grey horse had strained his leg and a miserable tramp had desecrated her carriage drive with his presence.

The old man had not even gained the footsteps when the doorman appeared and bade him begone, or else the dogs would be set on him. In vain the old fellow pleaded to see the lady of the house, saying that he was sure that she would at least give him some bread, for he was both hungry and penniless. But it was all to no purpose. With the lady's own words, "begging vagabond," repeated by her servant, ringing in his ears, he was turned away.

At the iron gates he stopped and gazed back with an earnest and peculiar look at the ivy-clad mansion in the distance. Then glancing towards the sky which was already darkening with night clouds, he said in a low, deep voice:

"Not there. Not there."

2

It was Christmas Eve in the great town. Snow lay on every roof. It was trampled into dirty slush on the pavement under the feet of the passers-by. The wheels of various carriages, carts and vans, with the heavy tread of their horses' hoofs, churned it to mud in the streets.

It was early evening, but already the shops were all lighted up, the street lamps shone brightly and the blinds were down in many of the private houses in the terraces and squares of the richer parts of the town; the warm cosy light of the fires, lamps and gas glowing through them accentuated the rawness of the atmosphere out of doors. Crowds of people were abroad finishing their Christmas shopping, posting letters with jolly red seals on them, and sending on great piles of parcels containing Christmas cards and presents for friends and relatives.

Many happy faces were to be seen among the passers-by. Good will and good humor towards all seemed to be the order of the evening in the busy streets. It was pleasant even to stand by and watch the people that Christmas Eve.

"God bless them all," thought an old wayworn man who entered the great busy town from the still country as the shades of night fell. But there was no warm fireside waiting for him; no smiling face to welcome him. He was a stranger and amongst strangers. It was too late in the day for him to obtain work, even if he had the strength to perform it, which he had not. He could only hope to find some charitable heart that might take pity on him and help.

He was unused to begging, so much was evident, for he did not stop the pedestrians with a plea for alms nor yet did he enter on the same errand the brightly-lighted shops which were so gay with Christmas cheer.

Perhaps he saw that the passers-by were too much occupied with their own concerns and the owners of the crowded shops too busily engaged making money to listen to his feeble voice. Again he did not go down the areas of the big private houses to ask charity from the servants who might have given him of their masters' goods, although he looked down several on his lonely way. He had met many repulses that day, and it is so easy to lose heart after repeated repulses and failures and to dread meeting more. Time after time he paused outside hall doors as if screwing up his courage to ask someone for help, but it always ended in creeping away without speaking, as if there was none to aid or care for him in all the world. Meanwhile, the night grew darker, the wind more keen, and the snow began to fall again in thick flakes.

At last he accosted a stout, red-faced, well-dressed man, who was standing on the steps of a handsome house in a suburban square to which his weary feet had wandered. This man had once been very poor, but was now a merchant prince. He was a self-made man. He had got on in the world through his own cleverness. He had made his tens and thousands and now rested on his laurels. The memory of his past penury was quite banished from his mind, and the knowledge of his present prosperity proudly filled its place. The fact that he had once known both cold and hunger did not soften his heart in the least to the poverty-stricken.

Instead, he was actually ashamed of having been born common and poor, and did all he could to forget it and pass for – what he never was and what he never could be – a gentleman. He certainly sent large sums occasionally to charitable institutions, but that was merely to have the pleasure of seeing his name in print, and to reap the praise of his fellow men. This was the person before whom the tramp paused and asked for alms on Christmas Eve.

What the poor soul pleaded for in his feeble voice was but a drop in the ocean of the rich man's wealth. But, alas, he asked at an unlucky moment. The merchant prince was awaiting the arrival of a Duke who was coming to spend Christmas with him. This was an honor which he had long desired. Of course his grace would ask him some time to his house in return for this hospitality, which invitation would mean a great lift into a higher social scale at once. Certainly it was very polite of his grace to hob-nob with him for this festive season, because he was in his debt for considerable sums of money, and would not be able to repay them for a long time yet to come, but who was to be any the wiser about that?

The rich man had asked his most influential friends to his house that day in order to meet this noble guest, so that it might be spread abroad that he mixed with the aristocracy of the land. But lo! just as his grace's carriage was in the very act of drawing up at the door, this wretched, tattered object was there begging for money. The Duke might think that he was on intimate terms with him, or if he had the slightest suspicion of his host's origin (and conscience makes cowards of us all) might think that he was related to him. Oh, horror!

"Go to the workhouse! For what else do we keep such an institution?" he roared. "Go away! Go away!"

Then pressing forward he poured hearty welcomes on his noble guests as he came up the steps. The two passed together into the warm, well-lit hall, the door was slammed, but not before the tramp heard the caustic voice of the merchant prince demanding:

"What do we pay the poor rates for?"

Once more the wanderer turned his tired face to the endless round of the streets. Ere he went, however, he cast on the house of the rich man the same peculiar look that he had given the noble country mansion. From that he looked up to the cold night sky and whispered: "Not there."

3

It was Christmas Eve in the slums of the great town. Dirt, noise, drunkenness and rowdy gaiety. Thinly-clad forms hurrying along with the few hardly-earned coppers – happy they if shillings – clenched in cold hands or shut up in shabby purses, with which to buy something for Christmas dinner.

The little shops, crowded with such poor customers, were as busy, if not busier, as the great shops in the richer streets. Some of these people had a smile on their worn faces, for was it not Christmas time, and with everything looking so bright and gay, it would be a shame to appear sour and sulky if one could possibly help it. Of course there were some who could not help it – and-God comfort them.

"All honor to these brave poor souls," murmured the weary wanderer as he came toiling down one of the meanest of the streets.

It was night now, a bitterly cold night. As yet he had found no shelter. He had trudged from the broad, brightly-lit roads of shops and houses to this squalid region, and here he often paused, stunned by the noise and confusion of the little streets, horrified by the bad language that occasionally met his ears, terrified by the sense of violence which now and then met his eyes, but nevertheless often cheered by seeing poor bright faces hurrying along, thinking more of others than themselves. One such face beamed on him as he passed a wretched little house situated in the midst of a squalid court. It was a man's face, a worn, thin, white face, but it had a kind smile on it for all that, a very kind smile, so kind indeed that encouraged the aged traveller to repeat his wish for a crust of bread and a shelter for the night.

The kind face looked doubtful, and its owner retired for a moment to confer with someone within the house. The old man, standing by the door, overheard what was said:

"He is worse off than we are. He has no roof over his head this bitter night while we still have this one. He is starving, old, and feeble, wife, and it's Christmas Eve." Thus the man.

A woman's soft voice instantly answered:

"Aye, 'tis Christmas Eve. Let him come in."

The kind face appeared again at the door, and invited him to enter.

Inside was a small room, which served as a kitchen, sitting room, and cobbler's shop all in one. A little fire burned in the grate, before which crouched three wee children, all poorly clad but very clean. On the table was one loaf of bread and a few hot potatoes. Some cracked cups, odd saucers and plates, and a brown teapot that glittered in the firelight, flanked by a jug of watery-looking milk, completed the preparations for a meal.

In the window stood a cobbler's bench. Everything in the room spoke of great poverty, but greater cleanliness. From the wife's thin gown to the snow-white table all was as clean and neat as willing hands could make it. The old man noticed especially the jam-pot filled with holly that adorned the humble board in honor of Christmas. The poverty-stricken owners of the room could afford no Christmas luxuries, but the red-berried holly was there to speak for the festive season.

"I should be glad of a crust and some water," said the guest as he looked round. "Then if I might pass this bitter night by your fire I should be so very grateful to you all. Cold is the night to the homeless and friendless."

The good wife nodded. There was something very pathetic about his words. God alone knew how poor they themselves were, and deep down in her heart lurked the secret fear that they, too, might soon be homeless and friendless. Therefore she could not refuse his request and turn him out again into the cold, bleak streets. Instead she heartily invited him to share the poor meal that they were just to partake of when he arrived.

After it was finished his weariness seemed to vanish as if by magic, and he gathered the children around him while the mother washed up the tea things and the cobbler set to work on a little shoe, endeavoring to make it somehow watertight. It was most extraordinary what good friends the old man became with those shy little children all at once. Why, it seemed as if they had known him all their lives. He played with them, taught them games, and sang to them until the little room rang with their laughter. It did the mother's heart good to see them so merry. But at last she had to interfere.

"It is nearly time for them to go to bed," she said with a note of warning in her voice. "I am afraid they will never sleep to-night, they are so excited."

"And that would never do," rejoined their visitor with a smile. "Now what shall I do to quieten down your wild spirits, my children? Ah, I know. I shall tell you a tale, and you must all be so silent while I tell it that one can hear a pin drop."

So saying, he took the youngest child in his arms and, seating the others on the bench beside him, he told them a wonderful tale of an angel who was sent down from heaven with the power of choosing someone on earth who was worthy to receive a special Christmas blessing from God. How that angel, knowing that he should be well served and made much of if he came in his robes of light, chose to appear in the likeness of a poor mortal. He told of the bad reception that the angel met with because he seemed poor, not much to look at, and simple in this world of craft and money worship, and how long he was in making his choice because he saw none quite worthy of the great gift he had to bestow. But at last he found a poor family who were very kind to him, even in the midst of their own deep poverty, and he chose them for the blessing which once received would never leave them, but continue to do them good for ever.

"A good story," said the father, as the old man concluded his tale. "But there are no such angels nowadays – worse luck."

His visitor regarded him intently for a moment, and then remarked:

"There are many angels in this world and many who will be angels, but your blind eyes know them not until they have passed home through the gates of death."

"I see them when I am asleep," said the youngest child, putting a thin little hand to pat his face.

"Don't tell stories, Agnes," said the mother, raising a warning finger.

The little one looked up at the old man and smiled, but

said nothing. He turned to the mother and asked earnestly:

"Why not? 'In heaven their angels do always behold the face of my Father, which is in heaven.'"

She grew red and looked at him uneasily as he kissed the child's small white face. She could not tell how it was, but deep down in her heart some sweet, solemn strain of heavenly music seemed to sound at that moment, and her eyes filled with tears. Hastily dashing them aside, she rose and said it was quite time for the children to go to bed. Obediently they left the room, but ere they went they insisted on kissing the old man good-night, and peculiarly beautiful was his smile as he kissed them and blessed them and watched them depart in the wake of their mother. The youngest alone paused to whisper:

"I do dream of the angels, old man."

He patted her head, and said quite as sincerely: "I know you do," while with a merry laugh she waved her hand to him and ran after the others.

"Agnes imagines things," said the father.

His guest made no comment, but merely asked his leave to lie down on some sacks by the still warm ashes of the fire, and was fast asleep by the time the mother returned from putting the little ones to bed.

Then the cobbler lay down the little shoe, for it was past mending. Sitting beside his wife at the other side of the hearth they talked together in low tones for fear of waking the sleeper. Their conversation told the story of their lives. They had come to the great town from a far-off country village near the sea in the hopes of bettering their position. But work was so scarce and workers so many that things had not prospered with them. They did not complain so much for themselves, now that they had fallen on hard times, but that the little ones should go cold, hungry and barefoot, was their greatest sorrow. They longed for the quiet green country again, for the dash of the waves on the seashore, the health-giving breezes of the hills. But there was no hope that they should ever be able to leave this noisy court and great city. Things were going from bad to worse with them, and as far as they could see, the New Year would be harder for them than the old one had been.

"But let us trust in God still," said the patient wife.

The husband nodded towards the quiet sleeper and added:

"Yes, wife. But for His goodness we might be like that poor soul was tonight, homeless and starving. It was that thought which made me ask him in."

A little more hopeful talk, and then they retired to an inner room to forget their troubles in slumber with their children.

4

It was Christmas Eve in Heaven. Before the Throne of Light stood an angel. His head was bowed in reverence, his great white winges closed.

"On whom shall I bestow the blessing?" asked a voice like that of many waters.

The angel turned his radiant face of everlasting youth and beauty towards that point in the vastness of space where this small planet of sorrow move silently on its ceaseless round, and said:

"On that poor cobbler and his family who shared their all with me when, as a ragged, hungry wayworn man, I asked their charity and was not refused."

"My blessing be on them, my peace, and great prosperity," replied the voice. And the mighty sound of a song of praise arose from the harps of Heaven.

On Christmas morning the cobbler and his family awoke to find the old man gone, how or where they know not, for the door had not been unlocked, nor was the window touched.

"He was the angel," said the little Agnes. But they only laughed at her. He had come into their lives and passed out of them again like a dream, but from that hour they prospered in all things. In the New Year an uncle of theirs, long unheard of and long since forgotten, died in Australia, leaving his entire fortune to the cobbler and his family. On receiving it they immediatly returned to the country village that they loved, there to open a business that prospered exceedingly under their hands. Three more little ones have since been added to their happy home circle, and cold, care and hunger are all things of the past. But little Agnes is no longer with them. She dreams no more of angels, for she has gone to be with them, and knows now who gave the blessing One Christmas Eve.

MADELINE CUMMINS (1912)

Mr. and Mrs.
Santa Claus

❦

DICK LENNON KNEW LIZZIE MURPHY just about as well as it is possible for a man to know a girl when he sees her only by the soft light of lamps or the yellow glamor of gaslight, or the white, dazzling brilliance of electricity.

There is no doubt that a few weeks at the same summer resort will enable people to understand each other's character far better than a whole winter season of dances and theatres, musicals and calls.

And Lizzie and Dick never met during the summer. Fate had decreed that with the first faint warmth of spring their ways should diverge and not come together again till the trees were leafless, and the earth cold and unsympathetic.

But for two winters they had attended the same dinners, the same receptions, the same theatre parties, and Dick had become a constant caller at her home.

Always there was an irresistible attraction between them, and when Lennon awakened to the fact that, whenever there was a possibility of their meeting, he was always looking for her and was conscious of a distinct sense of disappointment and discontent if he failed in his search, he became disturbed – for he felt that he did not know Lizzie as a man should know a woman he chooses for his wife.

She seemed to him but a beautiful dream-woman. He had never seen her except in evening dress. He could not associate her with anything real or practical.

They never met save in the artificial atmosphere of society life, where a woman's success depends upon her outward attractiveness. How could he know whether beneath that fair exterior, there was any sympathy, any thought of the deeper things of life; whether there was anything real in her, or was

90

she but a dainty butterfly, made to be looked at, and caring naught else than to flutter here and there and sip the sweets of every flower.

And then he confessed a little sadly to himself that whether she rose to the height of his ideal or fell far short of it, there never could be any other woman. She was his world.

If he could only know her a little better, he thought with a sigh.

It was Christmas Eve and there was a play in town in which both Lizzie and Lennon were interested. It was making but a short stay, and this was the only night on which their engagements would agree.

When he came in he found her looking over a book of Gibson's sketches which had been sent to her as a Christmas gift. Gibson was a favorite with him as well as with her and together they turned the pages, commenting and admiring and laughing at the quaint humor, when suddenly they came upon a picture entitled "A Christmas Fantasy."

Just a picture of a little newsboy asleep, huddled up on a stone step, the papers slipping from the loosened grasp of the tired little arm, and there, too, was the picture of his dream: a troop of toys and Christmas trinkets marching two by two up the page – horses and soldiers and drums and horns and all the other things that most delight a boy's heart.

As her eye fell on the page, the pity of it swept over her, the desolate look of the cold stone step, the lonely little fig-ure, the wistfulness of the little old young face, the thought of the brightness of the dream and the cheerless awakening.

With a stifled exclamation and a contraction of the eye-lids as from a sudden hurt, she placed her hand on the pic-ture as though she would shut out the sight of it; then closed the book and, rising hurriedly, crossed the room.

A look of surprise came into his face, and he, too, rose and followed her. As she glanced up at him, he saw that her eyes were filled with tears.

"What is it ?" he asked.

"I don't know. It hurt me somehow," she said, and stopped as though she found it difficult to go on; but he heard the quiver in her voice and was glad. He knew her better now.

With a little despairing gesture she said hurriedly: "It seems so real, so dreadfully real. I'm sure it is true; I'm sure there are hundreds of them. Oh, if I were not so helpless, if only I could do something! Of what use is it to give one's little meed of charity that goes one knows not where, and then go on living a life of utter selfishness and pleasure?"

A strange light came into his eyes.

"I'll tell you – " and then he hesitated. "What is it?" she said, turning towards him.

"I was going to suggest – but perhaps it wouldn't be practical. I was going to say, how would it be if we cut the theatre and went down to the heart of the town where the shops are? Perhaps we might find a little fellow or two that we could brighten up a bit. A wild idea, isn't it?" he finished up in an embarrassed sort of way.

"Wild?" she said with a great, wondering gladness in her face. "It is beautiful. Oh, could we, do you think? Mother won't mind, I'm sure. She had decided not to go tonight, anyway. It's quite early, and I shan't be a moment."

She moved swiftly to the door, stopped, turned half round and a flush rose to her brow. For one instant she wavered, and then came straight to him and looked up at him, with her chin tilted, but this time her eyes were very earnest.

"You must let me take my own money; you must let me pay just half," she said. "I shan't like it if you don't. It will seem as if I were doing nothing, and I shall feel just as selfish as before."

Lennon looked down at her and caught his lip between his teeth, and answered not one word.

A shadow of disappointment fell upon her face.

"Do you really mind?" she said, mistaking his silence.

"Mind?" and he laughed a little. "You shall do whatsoever it pleaseth you, my lady. You'd better run away now, but don't be long."

Presently he heard her step, and, glancing towards the door, a thrill of astonishment ran through him.

Could this trim, tailor-made girl in walking skirt, jacket and hat be really the same society woman he knew? He had forgotten that she would hardly go Christmas shopping in swirling draperies of silk and tulle.

He smiled down at her in a delighted sort of way. The dream-woman was charming, but this maiden was tangible; she was flesh and blood and there seemed to be something so companionable about her!

"And what will you do?" she said, glancing at his evening clothes. "We ought to look like the people we shall see, to be able to approach them."

"Oh, I'll turn up my overcoat collar and pull my hat over my eyes. Besides, you couldn't look like them if you tried a thousand years. How shall we go?"

"Well, dismiss the carrige, at any rate. We want to go among the people and get into the spirit of the thing."

The night was cold. A light snow was falling and the streets had just begun to whiten.

Lizzie and Dick alighted from a car in one of the busiest parts of the town, and started upon their search.

The streets were thronged with belated Christmas shoppers, hurrying to and fro, their arms filled with bundles, and each intent upon his own affairs.

Many and varied were the faces that passed. Some were pale and weary-eyed, others were ruddy and jovial; some were hard-featured and weather-beaten, many were careworn and thin; but all bore a certain look of expectancy, an indescribable something belonging to the time of year, a preoccupation that seemed to speak of home, and the hanging of stockings and delightful mystery and good will towards men; a sort of reflection from the inward glow of satisfaction that comes from the unselfish act of giving.

Lizzie and Dick had agreed upon taking turns. The first boy was to be Lizzie's property, the second Dick's, and so on. They had walked several squares, when, as they were passing a toy shop, Lizzie touched Dick's arm and they stopped.

Before the brilliantly lighted window stood an extremely small boy, very dirty, very ragged, and with that pathetically cold look about him that all small boys have when their sleeves are too short and their trouser pockets too small, and an expanse of red, chapped wrist thrusts itself uncompromisingly into view.

Lizzie looked at the shabby little figure and then at the dirty face, and saw there the same wistfulness as in that of the boy in the picture. Her hand went to her throat, and she whispered to Dick, "Speak to him. I can't yet."

Dick stood beside the boy for a little, pretending to look at the toys, and presently said quietly, "Well, old man, do you see anything in there worth having?"

The boy looked up at him, at first a little suspiciously, and then an awkward shyness seemed to come over him, and he shuffled his feet in the snow, kicked the grating, and made no reply. But, seeing that the tall figure with his collar turned up and his hat pulled over his eyes was not looking at him, but seemed to be absorbed in the toys, he plucked up courage and said, "I uz jes' a lookin' at dat 'spress waggin wid two horses an' boxes and t'ings. I uz wonder'n' wedder you cud onharness 'em."

"I was wondering that," exclaimed Lizzie hurriedly, "and I believe you can. See those buckles on the straps! Oh, I would like to see if I could do it, wouldn't you?" and she gazed longingly at the express wagon.

The small boy shuffled his feet again and replied: "'Taint no use a wishin'. Dem t'ings mus cos' a forchun."

"Oh, no, I don't believe they do. Suppose we go in and see. I do want to see if I can harness them up again, and then

you can take it home, for I'm too big to play with it."

The customers standing near looked on with amused interest as the extraordinary trio came in and demanded the express wagon, and Lizzie unharnessed the horses and pretended to forget how to harness them and made all sorts of mistakes, and the little fellow forgot his shyness and showed her how to do it, and they laughed with delight when they succeeded.

While Dick waited for the express, Lizzie and her charge went into the adjoining shop to find mittens and other little things to add to his comfort.

When they came out Dick had not yet appeared, and Lizzie sat down on the railing in front of the toy store and looked at the boy's face. It had lost its wistfulness and was shining with delight.

Lizzie smiled at him and put her hand on his shoulder. At the kindly touch he looked up at her in such a wondering way, as though it were something so strange, that all the motherliness of her nature went out to him.

He was alone in the streets on Christmas Eve, and he was so little and so uncared for. Suddenly she put both arms about him and drew him close to her, and put her face down against his dirty little cheek, and said with a break in her voice, "Good night, dear, and a happy Christmas to you," and then she became conscious that Dick was standing on the steps watching them.

She rose quickly and turned away, and Dick, with a few quiet words, delivered the precious toy into the boy's keeping, pressed something into his hand for the Christmas dinner and then joined Lizzie.

They walked on in silence. Lizzie's head was bowed a little so that the brim of her hat concealed her face, but he knew she was crying, and he was both glad and sorry – glad to find that she was truly womanly and sympathetic and sorry to have anything trouble her.

The rest of their trip was much the same, filled with

pathos and merriment, tears and laughter.

As they were nearing the end of their journey and were bidding farewell to a delightful ragamuffin whose arms they were filling with mysterious packages, a man passed them. He stared very hard as he went by and then turned square around and stared at them again before he passed on.

It was Laurence Casey, one of Lizzie's coterie of admirers and a college chum of her brother Tom's whom he was now on his way to see. When he reached the house he found that Tom had not yet come in, and sat down to wait for him.

The room was very dimly lighted. In a little while Lizzie and Dick arrived, and not noticing Casey, passed through to the rear apartment where the lamps were burning brightly.

He smiled to himself, and rose to go in and announce himself, when he saw Lizzie toss her wraps on a chair and go straight to Dick and look up at him with her chin tilted. Then he heard her say in a thrilling voice: "I don't know how to thank you. You were fine. I knew you would be like that."

And then Casey saw Dick take her face between his hands, and – but that was all he did see, for, recovering from his momentary paralysis, he grabbed his hat and softly closed the door after him.

In about half an hour he strolled into the club, and noting Jimmy Lacy lounging in a corner, he put his hand on his shoulder and said: "Well, Jimmy, I've bad news for you. Guess what I saw tonight."

"Can't imagine," rejoined Jimmy, "what was it?"

"Lizzie Murphy and Dick Lennon playing at Mr. and Mrs. Santa Claus, and, judging from that and – well, from other things, I think it's all up with us. What shall it be – suicide or supper?"

ANONYMOUS (1902)

Widow Dennehy's
Christmas Visitors

1

FAITH! 'TIS A FINE JOB I'VE MADE OF IT." The speaker was the Widow Dennehy, and the speech was made as she stood outside her cottage on Christmas Eve, admiring its improved appearance. Like most of her neighbors she had just whitewashed the front of her house and painted green the little shutters that closed the square windows at each side of the door. It was a troublesome task, but she wasn't going to be behind any of the inhabitants in the neatness of her home during the holiday season. And, here, it was done now, and done well, too. As she still stood contemplating with satisfaction the change she had wrought by her labor, a little cold shiver passed down her shoulders.

"Oh; it is cold," she muttered to herself. "The sky is very sullen-looking, and I'm sure we're going to have snow for Christmas."

She walked towards the door and gave a pleased glance at the interior, where her only daughter was busily engaged brightening up the delph and the furniture, and decorating the multitude of pictures that hung on the walls.

"Are you come to give me a hand, mother? I'd want it badly with this holly and ivy," said the daughter smilingly.

"I'll help you with a heart and a half, girl. And, sure, 'tis you're making the bright, cosy little kitchen of it."

In the old lady went, and set about breaking up the holly boughs into pieces suitable for the decorations.

As the old woman herself said, the kitchen was certainly a bright, cosy little one. Most of the cleaning had now been done and a clear burning lamp, with fancy glass chimney, threw a good blaze of light from its place on the chiffonier, that stood beside one of the walls. At another side a gleaming array of cups and saucers and plates and other ware attracted the eye, but most cheerful of all was the great coal fire crackling and flaming away in the polished fireplace. Its warm ruddy reflection was cast all around the room and imparted an impression of brightness and comfort that harmonized well with the traditionary happy associations of Christmas.

"This picture comes next for a Christmas wreath, mother," said the daughter from the chair on which she was standing to carry out decorations.

The picture she indicated was the well-known representation of Robert Emmet before his judges, and which occupied the place of honor over the fireplace.

"Give me a good piece of holly, mother, for brave Robert Emmet," said the girl, with a smile.

"Here you are – a nice, fine green bit, Nellie. He deserves it." And the mother handed up a good-sized, leafy branch of the evergreen, which the deft artistic hands of the daughter arranged very tastefully indeed above the picture of the patriot. But the process of adornment was hardly complete when,

"Tat-tat," came a knock suddenly at the door.

"The postman, as sure as I'm alive," said the mother, as she ran to open.

She was right in her guess. It was, indeed, a letter, and the writing showed to her delight that it was from her son, who was away at business in Dublin. She lost no time in getting her glasses and starting to read:

"Dear Mother – I'll be with you for Christmas. I have something very particular to tell you when I get home. A woman will probably call on you on Christmas Eve. Keep her till I come as she is a relation of mine. With love. – Your affectionate son,

"Jack"

"Is that all?" said the daughter.

"Not a single word more," said the mother, "of all the strange tantalizing letters a woman ever got, this beats 'em all hollow."

"'Tis terribly mysterious, as you say, Nellie. Why couldn't he tell us straight out what he has to tell like any ordinary Christian, instead of sending us a Christmas letter that's worse than a puzzle."

"'Twon't be the puzzle rightly for you, mother, until the strange woman appears on the scene."

"Faith! you're right there. I wonder from what corner of the land of Ireland will she come."

"There's no knowing. But you won't have long to wait, I suppose."

And she hadn't, for a somewhat timid rap was heard at the door at that moment.

"Talk of the devil, mother – you know the old saying. This is the stranger, for a ducat."

Mrs. Dennehy opened the door. A woman in a black hood cloak stood outside.

"Is Mrs. Dennehy within," asked the stranger.

"I'm the person, ma'am," said the widow, with a little smile of courtesy. "What can I do for you?"

"Well, I got a strange bit of a letter this morning, ma'am, and I can't understand it at all, at all. 'Tis signed, 'John Dennehy,' and I'm told to call here to you on Christmas Eve–."

Mrs. Dennehy perceived at once that this must be the strange woman who was to visit her, and to be kept until her son arrived.

"Come in, ma'am. Come in," said she, somewhat eagerly. She would now, she hoped, get all the explanation that was withheld in the short letter she had herself received.

In walked the strange woman, and throwing the hood back off her head, went towards the fireplace.

"Sit down by the fire, ma'am. I'm afraid it is going to be a cold Christmas."

"The snow is just starting to come down and it looks as if we were going to get plenty of it," said the visitor.

"Oh! then you must be perished alive. Sit down and make yourself comfortable, and Nellie, get a cup of tea ready as quick as you can."

And the daughter set to concoct the tea with the aid of the kettle that was sitting cheerily on the hob.

"But about this letter," queried the widow, as she scrutinized with no little interest the visitor who had now been placed in a chair in front of the merry blaze of the fire.

"Here it is," said the stranger, as she handed the missive over to the widow. "I'm afraid you won't get much information from it."

"'Tis from my son, sure enough," said the widow. "I got a letter also from him in which he told me to expect a visitor, and here you have come. But he didn't give one word of explanation – only sends this short note that excites curiosity instead of satisfying it. But, perhaps, your letter will tell us something."

"Faith! I have the same story to tell. My letter is quite as short and mysterious, ma'am. He couldn't be playing any joke on us?"

"Oh no! I know Jack too well to believe that for a moment. He just means whatever he writes, and you must stay till he comes. Indeed when my son invites you, you're quite welcome to my home."

"Thank you, ma'am. I'm sure of that."

The widow then read the second letter. It was just as the strange woman said – it told them nothing.

"Dear Mrs. Ryan," it ran, "I have something particular to tell you, and I want you to go over to my mother's house at the address I give below. Be there on Christmas Eve certain, and I promise you that you'll be very pleased to hear what I have to tell you. This seems a peculiar request from a stranger, but although I am a stranger, I can tell you that I am a relation of yours. So don't forget to come. – Your affectionate 'relation.' – John Dennehy."

"What's after coming over the boy at all?" said the widow, when she had read the letter, which only increased her curiosity four-fold.

"He talks about being a relation of mine," said the visitor, "but I never heard of any connection between our families."

Mrs. Dennehy had learned the stranger's name and address from the letter and agreed that there was no relationship whatever.

"I hope 'tis no mistake he's making," said the visitor with a touch of anxiety in her voice.

"He's not a lad for making mistakes," said the mother, with some little pride. "And anyway we'd better wait for an explanation till he comes himself. It can't be very long now till his arrival."

"That's the best thing, and the only thing to do," assented the visitor.

"Let us set to work with the holly and ivy in the meantime, mother, or we'll never have the place finished in time for the home-coming of this interesting son," said the daughter, archly. She had set an inviting tea on the table for the stranger and was now eager to get at her decorative work and complete it.

And away they started at the interrupted labor, carrying on the while a courteous conversation with their visitor, who was already proving herself very agreeable, and whom the widow had already taken a liking to, believing her to be a decent, respectable person.

But another interruption soon occured, in a totally unexpected maner.

2

The visitor was leisurely telling the widow how she, too, had a child in Dublin at business – a young woman of whom she gave a splendid account, when a busy knocking sounded at the door. The widow hurried forward and opened it.

Outside stood a small red-faced healthy-looking messenger boy. The snow, which was now falling steadily, covered his hat, and his gleaming oilcloth cape and boots.

"Is this where Mrs. Dennehy lives," he asked.

He was answered "yes."

"Then this parcel is for here," he said, and lifting up his cape, disclosed a great turkey, tied up in brown paper, but giving undoubted evidence of its protruding black feet.

"A turkey!" said Mrs. Dennehy, in great surprise, as she regarded with a humorous glance the messenger lad, holding out the parcel that was nearly as big as himself. "You're making some mistake, boy. I didn't order any turkey; take it back at once."

"This is the address I got, ma'am; and you'd better take it in. You may be sure there's no mistake."

"I'd better take the load off you for the present at any rate," she replied, as she allowed the parcel to be set down on the table, "but see that inquiries are made."

The parcel opened out as it was laid on the table, and wasn't it a grand bird – large and plump and white – just such a one as would look grand in a dish of steaming celery sauce at the head of a Christmas table.

"But there's no fear 'twill occupy a place on my table, and more's the pity," she murmured to herself.

The daughter and the visitor joined in the praise, but their remarks were drowned by another knocking at the door.

"Who on earth can be there now at all?"

Another messenger in oil cap and coat, and similarly liberally besprinkled with snow, was outside.

"Mrs. Dennehy here," said he, in a laconic query.

"Yes! 'Tis Mrs. Dennehy lives here."

"Then here's the ham that's been ordered," and he held out a parcel from which came the rich, savory smell of well-cured bacon.

"Are you sure you have the right address?" asked the widow.

"Perfectly sure, ma'am."

"But I didn't order any ham."

"Then it must have been ordered for you: you'll find there's no mistake," and he handed over the parcel.

"Better enquire further, however, before you make up your mind."

"Oh! I'm sure 'tis all right, ma'am," he said, as he walked away.

The widow stood for a moment looking out, and beheld all the busy indications of Christmas on the street. The farmers' carts were hurrying homewards with their noisy creaking, and the farmers' wives sitting cosily clothed in the well-filled butts. The streets and the houseroofs were covered with a great mantle of snow, while the lights beamed merrily out from all the houses and shops, and gave a gay appearance to the place. She was still looking with interest on all these features of the night when a heavily laden baker's van, with a pair of yellow lights in front like great big eyes, drove up. Down jumped the driver; over he ran to her door with a parcel.

"A happy Christmas to all within. Is this Mrs. Dennehy's?" he said briskly.

"This is the house," answered the widow.

"Then I have a very fine parcel for you, ma'am."

"Another parcel!" said the widow, with a worried look. "How many more are we to be bothered with?"

"Faith! 'tis very few, ma'am would have any objection to receive a splendid rich Christmas cake."

"Very few, I'm sure, if 'twas really intended for them, but then there's some blunder here. I didn't order it, and there's some big mistake. I'm afraid you'll be quickly driving back again for it."

"I don't think so, ma'am," said the cheerful driver. "You must have some thoughtful friend in town who remembered you for Christmas."

"I hardly think so," said the widow, and she doubtfully took over the cake and set it on the table. And it was a splendid one – brown and large – with a multitude of currants and raisins and pieces of citron and lemon peel   peeping out temptingly from the many cracks on its top.

And she wasn't yet done with the messengers. A great pile of groceries and biscuits and fruit and sweets arrived till Mrs. Dennehy began to be getting alarmed. She couldn't get out of her mind the feeling that there was some big mistake somewhere. No such wonderful pile of eatables had ever before reposed on her table, and 'twas with a feeling of sorrow that she contemplated them now, now thinking it such a pity that they should all probably have to go elsewhere after an hour and so.

"'Tis you have the fine tableful, God bless it," said the woman visitor, Mrs. Ryan, at length.

"'Tis a fine tableful that makes me anxious instead of glad, ma'am. The Lord only knows whom all the things belong to."

Just then the latch of the door was lifted and the door pushed in.

"I hope I'm in time to light the Christmas candle, mother."

The speaker was a tall, strong, handsome young man, and he uttered the words in a fine cheerful tone as he stepped in over the threshold."

"Jack! Jack! Welcome home, my boy," said the mother excitedly, running across to kiss the tall, strapping newcomer.

But she stepped up. Who was this entering behind? A very pretty, smiling young woman, and most surprising of all this young woman rushes into the arms of the stranger who had arrived earlier.

"Bessie! you here," said the latter, as she kissed the young woman with much show of affection.

"Yes, mother! Jack will tell you everything," and with an arch little smile she drew Jack forward.

"The story is a very short, simple one," said Jack. "I met a very nice charming girl in Dublin, and I asked her to be my wife – Bessie."

And he introduced her thus to his mother. The latter saw at once that he had gained just such a girl as she herself would have chosen for him and clasped her fondly to her breast.

"Welcome, and a happy future, my darling. And this is the secret, and the explanation. 'Tis ye were the pair of rogues to keep it from us."

"Oh! we meant no harm, mother," said Jack. "We said we'd not celebrate our wedding till we'd get home for Christmas, and we knew we'd give ye all a pleasant surprise when we'd come along and tell our secret."

At this, congratulations and kisses and explanations followed galore.

"I see," said Jack at length, "that all the parcels have turned up all right." And he glanced round at the goodly pile that lay on the table.

"Yerra! was it you sent them?" said the widow, rejoiced at this pleasing solution of her worries. "Faith! we were very near sending everyone of them back."

"Then our Christmas dinner has had a remarkable escape, mother," said Jack, with a laugh. "For all these things are ours. How else do you think we could celebrate suitably our wedding feast, deferred, as it is to this great occasion. We intend to celebrate our wedding and our Christmas together, and we mean to make it a right merry time."

And they did. And the widow Dennehy very quickly grew to love her little, smiling, happy daughter-in-law; and the best of humor during the whole of the Christmas season. He was here, there and everywhere, and he carved the great turkey, when it appeared steaming on the table on Christmas Day, with a skill that would have done credit to a hotel manager.

And as for songs – well! he made the little kitchen ring on Christmas night, and didn't he give "The Rising of the Moon" with splendid vigor and earnestness. And the wife sang, and the sister sang, and – the mother sang. Of course the mother said that she couldn't, and truly, she hadn't sung for many and many a long year, but Jack made her contribute some ancient song for this great occasion. 'Twas given in a shaky treble, but according to Jack's own words, "'twas worth travelling all the way from Dublin to hear."

The widow was a very happy woman, indeed, during those few days, and when she knelt down to pray to her God at Christmas Mass, her thanks were offered from a full heart that she should be given so much unexpected joy during the great season of "Peace and Good Will."

L. SULLIVAN (1907)

The Miser's Reward

1

THE SNOW DRIFTED along in heavy sheets, blown about in fantastic shapes by the icy blast as it swirled its way through a street of tumble-down houses in a tenement district in Dublin.

It was Christmas Eve, and, notwithstanding the severity of the weather, here and there a wayfarer crouched closer to the walls of the dilapidated houses in the hope of eluding the keen wind and the now thickening fall of snow as he made his way homeward. Lights shone in most of the windows, broken and patched as they were, and out of the squalor of the surroundings a merry laugh was now and again borne to the ears of the passer-by.

Down this street, with flagging step, and propelling himself along with a heavy stick, came an old man. The sickly flame of the lamps he passed under show up his sunken cheeks, protruding eyes and line-covered face. "A pest for the lot of you for a pack of fools, wasting your money on such nonsense," he muttered. "Christmas Eve! Bah! I can't afford any Christmas; if you kept your money to pay your rent 'twould serve you better, you fools. But I'll have no excuses from you; no, none." These observations were drawn from him by seeing a burly carter carrying a huge fowl into the doorway of one of the miserable dwellings, where he was greeted with howls of approbation and clapping of hands from a group of children. "Won it at the raffle, Kate, and dirt cheap for 3d., it is," he said passing it over to a worn-looking woman who appeared as if she would be unable to hold it from sheer weakness.

The old man stood to watch the scene, while the snow fell on his shoulders, then he strode up to the door. "See here, Mr. Murphy," he croaked, "I hope you have your rent all safe for me. To-morrow makes it two days overdue, and I'll come round for it, Christmas or no Christmas. It's either the rooms or the money I want; choose whichever you like. Isn't that a fowl I see there in your wife's hand?" he added. The carter was silent.

"Look here, Mr. Murphy, take that bird down to the poulterer at once and sell it to get me my rent," screamed the old man. "Fowl indeed! Such things are not for you and yours; it'll make you bilious, the lot of you," he sneered.

The carter stood forward, his oils glistening at the little group before him. "I tell you, Mr. Murphy, I'll call for my rent to-morrow, that is if I wait till then," was his determined answer.

"To-morrow, sir," echoed the carter.

"Yes," screamed the old man, "to-morrow, and why not. What is to-morrow to me any more than another day? Do what I tell you with that fowl and get me my rent," saying which he stretched his stick over and struck the bird which the woman held in her hands.

The carter looked at his wife, while the children, with hunger-pinched faces and eyes rivetted on the fowl, grasped their mother's thin skirt with their black and bony fingers, listening earnestly to what was being said. When their instinct told them the old man had designs on their treasure, they burst into dismal howls, which the carter gloomily silenced before he turned to the old man again.

"I can't see them starve, Mr. Crabbe, and it's all we have," he replied, waving his hand in the direction of the fowl.

The old man glared at him. "I'll be back again, Mr. Murphy, for my rent," he shouted over his shoulder as he turned away. Shuffling along the street he entered a tumble-down building, the windows of which were boarded up, and the whole appearance of which betokened utter desolation.

He passed along the wretched hall-way, which was in inky blackness, and ascended a rickety flight of stairs, the creaking and groaning of which, as he mounted it, broke the harsh sound of the whistling of the wind as it played mournfully with the shaky timbers of the decaying dwelling, and entered a small dark room, which contained a table, chair and a small wooden bed. His head shook as if he suffered from ague as he lighted a candle and peered cautiously around him. Searching carefully over the floor he picked up a piece of hard black bread, which he ate ravenously, washing it down with a long draught of water from a rusty tin can. He now locked the door carefully, and having listened for some minutes to the wind as it screamed round the house in a shrill key, knelt on the floor and burying his long horny finger-nails into a crevice in the boarding, slowly elevated a strip of wood, and disclosed, in the flickering light of the sputtering candle, the gleam of a heap of gold. Gazing apprehensively round him, his head shaking the while, he began to count the mass of sovereigns. For close on two hours he continued his task, and yet the pile had not perceptibly decreased as it lay in its aperture in the floor; then his weak body rebelled against the strain and he grew faint and ceased. He had yet, however, sufficient strength to fondle his treasure. This he did, lifting the sovereigns in his hands and allowing them to fall in sliding heaps around him until he was literally surrounded with gold.

Suddenly a sound fell on his ears. "What was that?" he muttered as he listened intently; "Like a step it sounded. Ugh! the wind blows this grand house of mine into a sorry plight – makes noises where none should be." Hastily blowing out the light he shoved the money back in the darkness, re-adjusted the board, and rose to his feet.

"Curses on that Murphy to have no rent for me to-morrow; but I'll force him. The others have paid up because they know me; they know old Richard Crabbe too well. They're on his property longer, and know he won't be fooled. It's not

too late yet, and I think I'll see him again and force him to sell the bird. Easy come, easy go; he won't miss it, not any more than if he hadn't won it," saying which Mr. Crabbe stumbled down the stairs, locked the hall door after him, and went out into the raging snowstorm.

2

The miserable street of houses which Mr. Crabbe owned and let out in rooms to the unfortunate creatures who had the misfortune to be his tenants stretched itself out before him as he ambled along in the snow. Arriving at the one in which Murphy occupied, a top back room, the old man entered the hall and shouted up the stairs: "Murphy, Murphy, the rent, the rent!"

The carter came down the stairs, speaking as he came, "I can't give it to you, Mr. Crabbe; "we had to buy fire and things, and I can't give it to you for two days."

"That won't do, Murphy; I'll have my rent now or I'll get a few men to take your furniture away to my house – that I will this very hour. Your rent was due two days ago – a full week's rent, and you know your agreement. Pay up now or I'll do what I say." The old man stood with his back to the wall waiting for the carter to speak.

"I can't give what I haven't got, Mr. Crabbe," replied Murphy.

Seeing the determination which was upon the old man's face, the carter went slowly upstairs, and after much talk between himself and his wife, and much crying on the part of the children, returned with the goose under his arm and stepped out into the snow, the old man hobbling after him. When he reached the head of the street the bright light of the poulterer's shop shone out across the snowy pavement and fell upon the wretched face of the carter and the self-satisfied one of Mr. Crabbe.

The poulterer, a stout, red-faced man, all buttoned up in

overalls, was weighing and parcelling as rapidly as he could, assisted by his wife and son. The carter stepped up to him. "I want to sell this bird," he said, while the old man stood blinking in the bright light and resting on his stick in the background. The poulterer took the fowl in his hands, turned it over, put it close to his nostrils, and finally threw it into the scales. "I'll give you 5s. for it, as it's a big one," he said.

The old man came forward. That'll do, that'll do; pay your rent, Murphy," he said with a leer. The carter took the five shillings in one hand, while he clenched the other as if he would have dashed it into the grinning face before him, but thinking better of it, he threw the silver into the outstretched hand of Mr. Crabbe. "May God forgive you," he said in a solemn way, and strode off with the snow falling hard and fast on him.

The old man counted the money twice, and carefully placing it in his pocket, disappeared up the street. So heavy was the snow falling that it was with the greatest difficulty he gained admittance to his tumble-down dwelling owing to the way the snow had clogged the door. He succeeded after a while, however, and presently found himself in his own room.

"I must get to bed quickly or not a doubt of it but I'll freeze to death," he muttered. "I'll warrant these Murphy people have a fire to-night, aye, and a big one roaring up the chimney." He stretched out his long thin hands as if he would warm them at some imaginary fire as he spoke, then quietly removing his well-worn garments, jumped into bed.

The wind moaned piteously around the house, playing weird pranks with every loose brick and tile, and rattling the shaky window sashes until the old place seemed full of noises from the attic to cellar. Richard Crabbe, lying in bed, heard it whistle low, rise gradually, and shrieking loudly, die away in a faint wail; but above the din of the storm he heard the bells ring out their glad tidings of "Peace on earth, goodwill to men." A queer feeling was upon him, of which he knew not what to make. He thought of the sound he had heard earlier in the evening; he thought of Murphy finding it so hard to part with his fowl; he thought of Christmas Day and of how he would spend it. "Better than most people," he muttered, "counting my money, counting my money," and unable to control his hungering eyes longer from feasting on his gold, he rose from his bed, and lighting the stump of a candle, stumbled across the room. "The light shows too much, too much," he repeated, and gazing round to make sure no eye was upon him, he blew it out and dropped on his knees to the floor where he fumbled for some minutes. Suddenly a long shrill scream like that of an animal with its death wound, broke in the air, and Richard Crabbe jumped to his feet, and with quaking fingers and ashen lips, relighted the stump and candle and peered into the hole. The gold was gone – the big heap of yellow glistening sovereigns had disappeared – not one remained. In their place was a roughly scrawled note, which he read with chattering teeth and head shaking from side to side. It ran thus:

"Dere Mister Miser – Ye went out at the rite time to-night. I got the gold safely stowed away, and passed you with it on me back as you were so kindly getting a fowl for yer friend at the top of the street.

"Dan Smart"

Richard Crabbe rose from his stooping posture to his feet and allowed the slip of paper to flutter from his benumbed fingers. So great was the shock that for some moments he was unable to do more than grope about; then the storm of rage broke, and he frothed out of the mouth. His face grew black, and the veins stood thick in his forehead; he twisted his arms and legs until they cracked; but nature intervened at last, and the wretched creature finally broke a blood vessel.

They found him the day afterwards beside where his hoard once lay, and buried him at the expense of the city.

•   •   •   •   •   •

There had been one witness of the scene between the

carter and old Richard Crabbe as they stood in the wretched tenement doorway on Christmas Eve night – this was old Father Tom Dolan, the kindliest priest on the north side of the city of Dublin. He had listened to what had taken place between Crabbe and the carter, and having heard all, had slipped quietly away, taking a note of the number of the house as he went.

The following morning as the carter was gloomily ruminating the loss of his Christmas dinner, a loud knocking sounded on the door. Hastily rising and opening it, he was confronted by a boy who carried a hamper on his shoulder.

"Are you Mr. Murphy?" inquired the lad.

"I am," replied the carter, gazing at the hamper wistfully.

"This is for you," said the boy, laying his burden inside the door and clattering down the stairs.

In great amazement Murphy and his wfe set about opening his unexpected hamper, while the children stood round and clapped their hands for joy.

And such a hamper it was! There was a big goose, the materials for a substantial pudding, and a large Christmas cake.

It was a happy family who sat down to dinner that Christmas day in Murphy's modest home. There we will leave them, joyous and thankful, wishing each other what the writer sincerely wishes the reader of this little tale, A Happy Christmas and a Prosperous New Year.

B. J. K. Quinn (1907)

Gobble, Gobble

I N COUNTY SLIGO, far west, within sight and sound of the booming ocean, and in the heart of a comfortable farming district, there lived, some years ago, the renowned Bill Davy and his wife. No! They had no children – which was an unusual state of affairs for that part of the world – just cows and pigs, hens, ducks, geese, sometimes turkeys, and the beloved strip of earth of which Bill was the proud, if somewhat careless, lord and master.

Now, Bill did not hold that the patient cultivation of the soil and the eternal round of "hopping and trotting," as he called it, inseparable from farmwork, was quite the thing for a man of his abilities. Perhaps this was the reason why his little estate was not quite as trim as it might have been, and why the "brass" did not come rolling in as quickly as Bill – or any of us for that matter – would like to see it.

But if he didn't put the shoulder to the wheel with the same ferocious determination as the rest of the neighbors, who are an awe-inspiring example to the world, in this direction, he spent many a weary hour trying to hit on some scheme out of which he hoped to squeeze a golden shower, and thereby save himself the disagreeable necessity of wringing a living from the land.

So far he had not succeeded in bringing such a happy idea to fruition, though he had made several gallant attempts, perhaps the most noteworthy being his purchase of a goodly consignment of coffins which he proposed selling at a fair profit. He might have done so, given the necessary time, but Mary (that was his wife's name) so strongly objected to the presence of coffins in every room of the house that before even one of the neighbors was obliging enough to die, he was glad to resell the lot to a chap in town for something considerably under cost price. This rebuff very nearly decided Bill against further incursions in the commercial world, but the fact that Christmas was drawing near, coupled with the depressing knowledge that money was disgustingly scarce, set his inventive genius at work once more.

Behold our hefty hero, therefore, one grey December morning seated on his own special three-legged stool, his broad back propped against the white-washed wall of his ancestral home, blowing fragrant clouds of metamorphosed plug in all directions, and giving an occasional distracted scratch to the bald desert on top of his head.

Mary, who read the signs and tokens aright (as well she might, seeing the practice she had at that same spot since she married his lordship nigh on thirty years before) nodded quietly as one who should say, "He's got them again," and enquired in her patient voice: "What is it this time, avic?"

Her better half forthwith emitted the very father of a grunt, took the puffing Billy from between his teeth, and with a gravity that would have sat well on Solomon himself, gave voice to his thoughts:

"At last, Mary, I've thought of a sure plan for making a little bit quick and easy. It's a wonder I didn't think of it before. I'll start buying geese and turkeys and send them off to England for the Christmas. I know a firm that will buy from me, and the neighbors will be glad to send me their birds and wait for the money till my check arrives." (There was no fuss about shippers' licenses and nonsense of that kind in those good old by-gone days.)

Now, Mary was wise as women go, and well knew that to argue with a man of Bill's make-up was inviting trouble, so she contented herself with a faint sigh and a gentle lifting of tired eyes to the kitchen rafters.

Always the boy for striking the iron while 'twas hot, Bill lost no time in further deliberations, but immediately clattered off to the neighboring farms, where the wares in which he intended to trade were to be had at bargain prices.

A rumbling noise brought Mary to the little "look-out"

Sheila
Kern

window of the tiny porch a few hours later. To her amazement she beheld a long procession of despondent donkeys
approaching, all drawing seemingly heavy cargoes of the
unfortunate bipeds, whose opinions of the affair were
uttered in a very decided, if somewhat, undignified manner.
At their head trod Bill triumphant, gesticulating, encourag-
ing, finally marshalling them into some sort of order round
the barn door, where the work of unloading commenced.
Who shall describe the ensuing hour? What frightful squawks
from the terrified geese, what unearthly gobbles from the
indignant turkey-cocks; what lusty bellows from the perspir-
ing helpers when some refractory quadruped showed a dis-
position to wander from the stirring scene; what delighted
yelps from the dogs that thought the show was got up in their
exclusive interests, and made frantic snaps at each bundle of
feathers as it was hauled into view!

It was with hope running high and plans made for the
dispatching of the cargo the following day that Bill retired to
rest that night. Just as the first delicious heaviness descended
upon him, rude sounds of disagreement amongst the feath-
ered captives – at time reaching an astonishing pitch – gradually filled his soul with an almost uncontrollable fury, so that
by the time daylight came he arose, and very much in the
mood for it, commenced the devastating task of breaking
their b—— necks.

The work of packing and transference to the railway station having been accomplished, Bill spent several anxious
days awaiting news of the safe arrival of his consignment. It
came, as did also a check that delighted the very eyes of our
enterprising hero.

This happy climax, of course, determined the now boast-
ful Bill on immediately trying his hand at the game again.

Mary ventured to point out that at present the barn was
filled with unthreshed oats, that she strongly objected to
being kept awake at night by battling bipeds, that the whole
thing was getting on Bill's brain, and that he had better

attend to some of the farmwork which was sadly falling into arrears. His parting words that evening showed, however, what Bill thought of talk like that:

"I'm off to Kelly's now for a game of twenty-five, and I'll make the bargain for his lot if he's anyway responsible about the price."

After his departure Mary sat for some time gazing moodily into the bright embers of the turf fire. Presently a slow smile passed over the usual stern gravity of her countenance. Rising she set about performing the usual nightly tasks – getting in the turf and water, milking the cows, boiling the porridge for supper, tidying up the house – all of which took a much longer time than it takes to tell.

Close on twelve o'clock she went to the hen-house and fetched from it their old turkey-cock, whose gobble was a thing of beauty considered for volume alone. To his hoary leg she attached a piece of stout cord; then wrapping her shawl around her shoulders and turning down the light she went out of doors carrying old "Coaching Harry" under her arm.

About the very same hour found Bill standing in Kelly's doorway saying a cheerful "good-night," and repeating his intentions of coming round for the turkeys in the morning. His thoughts dwelt with proud satisfaction on the nimble way in which he had brought Kelly's original demand for the turkeys down to about a half, as he hammered home his hurried way. The night was rather dark, but calm; the road was quite deserted, lights were out in all the neighbors' houses, so that Bill began to feel a little bit queer as he approached a spot locally known as "The Two Bushes," where a monstrous turkey-cock was supposed to appear at certain times to those of whose habits of life it disapproved.

As he came almost abreast of the first of the "Two Bushes" a slight sound drew his eyes upward and with a spasm of horror, poor Bill saw the fabled creature silhouetted on the top of the ditch, poised in readiness to spring upon him.

Transfixed, he gazed open-mouthed, but when the monstrosity actually jumped in his path, emitting a horrifying "Gobble Gobble," Bill, brave as he was, turned tail and fled back to Kelly's, refusing to budge until Kelly agreed to escort him home with a lantern.

Meanwhile, Mary had returned the scandalized turkeycock to his perch, hurriedly put out the light and retired to rest. Under the window she heard Bill's "good-night" to Kelly.

"Thanks for coming with me," he said; "but after what I've seen to-night I think I'll have no more to do with turkeys, so you'll have to find another buyer. Don't mention what I told you to anybody, like a good man. I don't want Mary to hear it."

Mary could not help but admire Bill's bluff, when next day he explained to her why he had decided to retire from commercial life, for the present at any rate.

"Don't you see that the barn is filled with oats, and the work is all behind hand, and you don't like the gobbling and crackling, and I thought it would please you more if I stuck to the farming a bit more? – well, that's why I didn't buy Kelly's lot last night."

"Oh, I see," said Mary, and, being a woman of few words, left it at that.

M. REDICAN (1930)

The Black Dog

❦

I N THE YEAR 1808 on a Christmas Eve night the "Coach and Horses," an old–time inn or small hotel, which lay on the outskirts of Dublin, facing the northern road, had a goodly number of visitors, who had been forced by the inclemency of the weather to seek refuge within its hospitable walls. The folk said that such a night had not been known for many years; and when one looked at the immense snowdrifts which blew in walls of whiteness against the inn door there was no more evidence required to prove it.

The coach from the metropolis with its freight of passengers bound for their different Christmas firesides had reluctantly had to pull up at the "Coach and Horses," where they now sat around a big fire gazing comfortably into its ruddy depths while they listened to the beating of the snow and the moan of the wind without. Time and again an impatient passenger would rise from his seat and, brushing the moisture from the inside of the windowpanes, would peer out on the whiteness in the vain hope that there might be some abatement in the fierceness of the storm, but would return again to his place at the fire with sombre face telling of the fact that there was no cessation in the snowstorm.

The night wore on without a break in the keen hiss of the falling snow as the cruel wind blew it hither and thither in great drifts. It was near midnight when the host of the inn, who had been up to this time superintending the preparation of supper, came to join his guests in the comfortable parlor.

"A bad night, ladies and gentlemen, a very bad night, and but scant hope of a break, I'm sorry to say," he said rubbing his hands briskly. The guests murmured in agreement with him, some of them plaintively. One of them, a stout comfortable farmer, suggested that the party should imagine

123

themselves at home, and prepare to have their Christmas dinner at the inn on the morrow. He would, he said, take the head of the table, and winking at a pretty young girl who sat with her mother near the fire, and who was youthful enough to be his daughter, suggested she should take the other end, and between them they would take the part of the host and hostess to the snowbound passengers. At this there was much merriment, the farmer joining heartily, while the young girl, finding all eyes directed towards her, blushed and shook her head.

After many pleasantries of this kind had been exchanged there came, as there always will come in the jolliest party, a lull in the conversation, and someone suggested that each member of the party should tell a story. By universal aggreement it was decided that the landlord should begin, and without further ado that worthy lay back in his chair and gazing into the fire for a little while as if to collect his thoughts, began as follows: –

"There is a strange tradition attached to the portion of the country, which I don't suppose any of you have ever heard: that being so it will make my story all the more interesting. Close on fifty years ago on Christmas Eve night there came to this inn, which was at that time kept by my father, a traveller, who had with him a large black dog. It was a fearful night, and with the enormous fall of snow, which had been coming down for four days, the road was impassible. This gentleman's name was Richard Moore, and I believe he was a barrister practicing at the Irish Bar. He was a young man, tall and handsome, and was on his way home to spend Christmas with his father and mother, but was stopped owing to the heavy condition of the roads. After he had had his supper he expressed himself as being unable to sleep, and calling to his dog, he passed out of the inn with the intention of seeing how the night went before going to bed. You see he had been riding all day, and may have felt stiff and glad of stretching his legs, though how he meant to walk on such

roads was only known to himself.

An hour passed away and yet another, but there was no sign of Mr. Moore, and my father being unwell at the time, was forced to close the inn and go to bed, although he was ready at the first knock to hasten from bed and let him in. My father must have dozed asleep as he was awakened by a noise at the inn door. Coming down the stairs quickly he seized an old musket which hung in his room, in case of robbers. After asking who was there and getting no reply, he opened the door. Then a great black mass bounded on top of him. My father fired with the best aim he could and his shouts brought two servants running. After the lights had been lighted, they discovered that it was the traveller's dog. The dog appeared to be dead and so my father threw it outside the door. He knew that the dog's coming boded no good, but as the night had become more inclement there was nothing he could do about it.

You can imagine my father's surprise when he learned next morning that the dead body of the traveller had been discovered and beside it lay the dead dog. The dog must have regained consciousness, being only stunned by the shot, and wandered off to his master's side. It was said that the black dog had been seen since in the neighborhood on Christmas Eve nights, especially snowy ones. How true this is I do not know."

Just as the landlord had concluded his story a great whirl of wind swept around the inn, and lashing itself with a fierce bellow against the door of the porch, snapped the fastening and blew it back on its hinges, at the same time extinguishing the candles, which were placed at different intervals in the old-fashioned parlor. As the candles went out, the glow of the fire lit surroundings with fitful gleams. It shone on the faces of the travellers and quickly left them in darkness again.

There was an attempt made on the part of those nearest the door to shut it, then a confused murmur of voices, and all the travellers sat peering, awe-struck at the thing in the door.

The fire burned up brightly, and as it flared up, the eyes of the travellers were fixed on the form of a large black dog. Its red tongue lolled out between its white fangs, and it turned its head mournfully from side to side as if in entreaty. The blaze sank as rapidly as it had risen and plunged the parlor into darkness. When it rose again the dog had disappeared. A murmur rose from all in the parlor and each one rose from his seat. The landlord was the first to jump from his seat and called loudly for lanterns, which were quickly brought. He seized one and rushed through the door, followed by all the male members of the party, all either carrying sticks or lights. Out in the dark night they ran, in pursuit of the dog, which scampered before them, and its black body was easily defined against the snowy ground. At the main road the dog disappeared and left its followers bewildered. They beat the surrounding bushes in a vain attempt to find the dog.

Suddenly one of the party shouted and in a short time he was joined by all. On the ground in front of them was the lifeless body of a man in the exact spot where the dog disappeared. Finally they reached the inn and after much chaffing of hands and feet and administering warm drinks, the man opened his eyes.

After some hours' rest he was able to join the others and drink a toast to the timely warning of the Black Dog. He told the party that he had fallen off his horse that morning, and after travelling for some distance, that on foot he was overcome by fatigue and fell down on the roadside.

Towards morning the snowstorm abated and the party was enabled to continue its journey to their own Christmas firesides.

DEE CULAN (1934)

Index

"Adeste Fideles," 21
Angels, 86, 87, 88

Barmbrack, 7, 8, 12, 13, 14
Boxes, Christmas, 14, 16

Cake, Christmas, 105, 106, 116
Candlelight, breakfast by, 7
Candles, Christmas, 9, 39, 41
Cards, Christmas, 20, 81
Charms, silver, 10
Clothing, customs regarding, 8, 9
Clubs, Christmas, 22-30
Crackers, Christmas, 35

Decorations, 98, 99, 103
Dinner, Christmas, 41, 57, 84, 96,
    107, 116, 124
Dreams, 26, 27, 60-65, 91
Drunkenness, 37-38, 58-60, 68-71,
    75, 84

Games, party, 32, 36
Geese, 16, 20, 113, 118
Gifts, 9, 30, 47, 57, 81, 91

Ham, 12, 44, 105
Hampers, Christmas, 22-30, 116
Holly: 42, 72, 85, 98, 99, 103;
    superstitions regarding, 9
Housekeeping: 85, 98;
    customs regarding, 8
Household lore, 7-9
Hyms, 21

Ivy, 98, 103

Light, giving away, 9

Little Christmas cake, 8
Luck, Christmas and, 9-10

Mass, Christmas, 14, 44, 198
Messengers, Christmas, 104-106
Mince-pies, 9, 10
Misers, 22-30, 104-16
Mistletoe, 9, 42

Parties, 32, 34-37
Plum pudding: 12, 20, 21, 57, 59,
    60, 61, 62, 65;
    superstitions regarding, 10, 11
Priests, 23, 24, 116
Pudding, Christmas, 57, 116

Raffles, Christmas, 22, 23, 72, 76
Roses, Christmas, 30, 49, 50, 53,
    54, 56

St. Stephen's Day, 65
Shopping, Christmas, 47, 67, 68,
    78, 81, 84, 93
Snow, 42, 77, 81, 82, 93, 94, 98,
    105, 109, 113, 114, 123-27
Stockings, hanging, 94
Stuffing, bread and onion, 15
Superstitions, 7-9

Toy shops, 94-96
Turkeys, 15, 29, 44, 104, 108, 118,
    120, 121
Trees, Christmas, 62
Twelfth Day, 7, 8

Whiskey, 23, 27, 31, 33, 35, 37,
    58, 62, 67, 72, 74, 75
Wise Men from the East, 10